EXTREME VIRTUES

D1157987

EXTREME VIRTUES

Living on the Prophetic Edge

DAVID FILLINGIM

Foreword by
Glen H. Stassen

Herald
Press

Scottdale, Pennsylvania
Waterloo, Ontario

Library of Congress Cataloging-in-Publication Data

Fillingim, David, 1960-
    Extreme virtues : living on the prophetic edge / David Fillingim.
    p. cm.
    Includes bibliographical references.
    ISBN 0-8361-9235-4 (pbk. : alk. paper)
    1. Christian life—Biblical teaching. 2. Virtues—Biblical teaching.
    3. Bible. O.T. Prophets—Criticism, interpretation, etc. I. Title.
    BS1199.C43F55 2003
    241'.4—dc21

                                                        2002155510

EXTREME VIRTUES
Copyright © 2003 by Herald Press, Scottdale, Pa. 15683
    Published simultaneously in Canada by Herald Press,
    Waterloo, Ont. N2L 6H7. All rights reserved
Library of Congress Catalog Card Number: 2002155510
International Standard Book Number: 0-8361-9235-4
Printed in the United States of America
Book and cover design by Merrill R. Miller
Cover photo: Eyewire

10 09 08 07 06 05 04 03 10 9 8 7 6 5 4 3 2 1

To order or request information, please call
1-800-759-4447 (individuals); 1-800-245-7894 (trade).
Website: www.mph.org

Contents

Foreword

i think David Fillingim may be the next generation's Richard Foster, Dallas Willard, or Marva Dawn. He writes so very well, and he moves us so much—to growth and deepening, and to rejoicing at the little mustard seeds called forth in our living when we read him. And at the same time, there is a deep strand of realism in his spirituality, akin to the prophets and to Jesus. I know David Fillingim in his own family responsibilities and steadfast love, and in his own deep, deep caring. This is the voice of a genuine disciple of Jesus that you are about to read. Read and turn.

It is marvelously striking how the spirituality that David describes, which he roots in the prophets, and most frequently Isaiah, is so very much like the spirituality of Jesus. And indeed many of us are discovering how often Jesus refers to the prophet Isaiah, and the Psalms, more often than any other book. Jesus is very much in the tradition of Isaiah, and David Fillingim is very much in the tradition of Isaiah and Jesus. Extreme Virtues is truly incarnational discipleship.

As David Fillingim points to Isaiah and the other prophets, he is readying us to understand Jesus more deeply. This is the point I want to make. As David says, we need to understand that the prophets were not just predicting the future, or only confronting what was wrong. As David writes, "The biblical prophets were primarily oriented toward the present." Isaiah especially, not only confronted wrong, but proclaimed the hope that God would bring God's reign and deliverance. This hope is what Jesus proclaimed and enacted.

David writes that "the kind of worship that pleases God consists of justice for the oppressed, food for the hungry, shelter for the homeless, clothing for the naked." This is exactly what Jesus proclaimed in Matthew 25 and throughout his ministry.

David points out that Hosea sums up God's priorities: "For I desire steadfast love and not sacrifice, the knowledge of God rather than burnt offerings" (Hos. 6:6). Jesus makes the same point and quotes the same passage from Hosea in Matthew 9:13, and again in Matthew 12:7.

David shows how Jesus echoes the words of Amos and the other prophets about our responsibility for what we do and how we judge others: "Do not judge, so that you may not be judged. For with the judgment you make you will be judged, and the measure you give will be the measure you get" (Matt. 7:1-2).

"The specific sins Amos and the other prophets most often condemn are sins related to the failure to take adequate responsibility for weaker members of the community." So Jesus regularly goes to the outcasts and the dominated, and says he came not to heal those who are well, but those who are sick.

David writes: "Biblical justice is not merely distributive; it is restorative. Biblical justice aims at restoring the marginalized to full participation in the community." So Jesus was always bringing in the outcasts and practicing table fellowship with them, healing the blind and lame and restoring them to full participation in community, touching the untouchable, and making women full and responsible participants in the community of the witnesses and proclaimers of the gospel of the cross and the resurrection.

As David says, Jesus echoes Amos and Micah in pronouncing blessings on the poor and curses on the wealthy in Luke 6:20-21, 24-25.

> Blessed are you who are poor,
> for yours is the kingdom of God.
> Blessed are you who are hungry now,
> for you will be filled. . . .

Based on the prophets, David declares: "If we do love God, then we love God wholeheartedly. The paradox is that, though steadfast love for God is exclusive, steadfast love when directed toward other people is inclusive. Our love for our neighbors is rooted in and reflects God's love for us and our neighbors." Just so Jesus said, ". . . you shall love the Lord your God with all your heart, and with all your soul, and with all your mind, and with all your strength. The second is this, 'You shall love your neighbor as yourself.' There is no other commandment greater than these" (Mark 12:29-31).

"We live in a world where authentic hope is difficult to come by," writes David. But he gives us hope, citing the prophet Isaiah, prophesying hope. Such hope is what Jesus proclaimed: the hope and reality of the coming of the kingdom of God. And when he proclaimed the kingdom of God and its hope, he regularly cited the prophet Isaiah, even as David does. It is no accident that David and Malinda named their daughter Hope. They and Hope are in the tradition of Isaiah and Jesus.

"Isaiah had the courage to speak forthrightly to the king on sensitive matters of foreign policy with a perspective that contradicted popular opinion." Jesus had the courage to speak forty times in the Gospels in confrontation of the Sadducees, Pharisees, Scribes, wealthy—the powers that ruled daily life in Israel—with a perspective that contradicted their injustices.

"By God's power, Micah possessed the courage to speak forthrightly about the sins of God's people and their disastrous consequences, which would include the unimaginable tragedy of the destruction of Jerusalem." And so, of course, did Jesus. He wept over Jerusalem as he spoke of their not knowing the practices that make for peace, and he predicted the destruction of the Temple and Jerusalem.

David concludes with the virtue of peacemaking, quoting Isaiah and Jesus:

They shall beat their swords into plowshares,
    and their spears into pruning hooks;
nation shall not lift up sword against nation,
    neither shall they learn war any more. (Isa. 2:4)

Blessed are the peacemakers, for they will be called children of God. (Matt. 5:9)

David Fillingim, bringing us into the spirituality of the prophets, and especially Isaiah, is bringing us into the tradition of Jesus.

—*Glen H. Stassen*
Fuller Theological Seminary

Acknowledgments

many people have contributed to this book, including all the people I've known and admired over the years as exemplars of what it means to live a faithful life of service to God and God's people. Obviously, I can't name them all. But I would like to acknowledge my debts to a few of the people who had a special role in this book becoming a reality.

First, I'd like to thank Henlee Barnette for demonstrating that it is indeed possible to be both a Baptist and a prophet at the same time. From all of us, Henlee, thanks for the ice cream.

Second, I'd like to thank the good people of Potecasi Baptist Church in Potecasi, North Carolina—among whom the idea for this book was born—for their hospitality, love, and prayers.

I'd like to thank my wife, Malinda, and my daughters, Hope and Hannah, for loving me when I am virtuous and when I am not. Hope and Hannah have been constant reminders of the virtues of hope and courage. Malinda has been my loving partner in life and ministry, and has shown me what the virtue of steadfast love is all about.

Finally, I'd like to thank Sarah Kehrberg of Herald Press for her kind and careful editing, which has resulted in a better book than the one I originally composed.

Introduction

WHY I AM NOT A MODERATE

are you a conservative or a moderate?" I've often been asked.

I always answer, "No."

In Southern Baptist circles the question invariably arises, since Southern Baptists have divided themselves into these two camps over the last two decades. What my questioners are seeking, of course, is a quick and easy way to determine where my loyalties lie. But most questions worth answering do not have simple answers. And so, at the risk of appearing evasive, I simply answer "no" and leave them with puzzled looks on their faces.

But I'm not merely being evasive. If asked whether I am a conservative or a moderate, the correct answer is indeed "no."

I believe in conserving what ought to be conserved, but I am not of the particular political affiliation that Southern Baptists have come to associate with the term conservative. And conservative is such a relative term anyway. I'm much more conservative than many of the professors I meet at academic conferences. Yet a good number of my students seem to think of me as liberal. So conservative is not a label I can meaningfully claim.

But neither can I call myself moderate. I have some beliefs in common with the Baptist group known by that name—most notably, an opposition to fundamentalist efforts to proscribe the roles of women in the church. But the bourgeois values of the suburban churches and small-town "First" churches that make up the moderate Baptist networks and organizations are not my values. In fact, I've come to hate the word moderate.

Soon after the conservative/fundamentalist takeover of the Southern Baptist Convention in the early 1980s, Southern Baptists who opposed the fundamentalist movement began to call themselves moderates. The term was intended, first, to refute the fundamentalist accusation that the moderates were really liberals, and second, to soften upper-middle-class Baptists' embarrassment at being associated with highly publicized, distasteful fundamentalist antics, such as Southern Baptist Convention president Bailey Smith's assertion that God doesn't hear the prayers of Jews. In calling themselves moderate, non-fundamentalist Baptists were saying, in effect, "Yes, we're Baptist, but we're not like those extremists. We're part of polite society. We believe in education and progress. We live in the twentieth century, not the nineteenth." Calling myself moderate would be primarily an effort to define my identity by what I am *not* (I am not liberal or fundamentalist) rather than by what I *am*.

The Practical Value of Moderation

The principle of moderation is not a new idea. It has a long and distinguished history. In ancient Greece, the philosopher Aristotle defined moderation as the essence of virtue. Aristotle thought that the purpose of human life is happiness, and that the way to achieve happiness is to bring all of life under the control of reason. The mechanism by which reason controls human behavior, Aristotle believed, is moderation.

Aristotle observed that people pursue happiness through a variety of activities, and that people can and often do engage in activities to the point of excess. On the other hand, Aristotle also noted that people can be deficient in the degree to which they engage in any activity. Excess and deficiency can also characterize people's attitudes or dispositions. But between deficiency and excess stands virtue—just the right amount, the moderate amount—of every activity or trait. For example, a person with too much self-confidence is foolhardy or reckless. Foolhardiness or recklessness is a vice. On the other hand, a person deficient in confidence is a coward, and cowardice is also a vice. But in between cowardice and recklessness stands the desired moderate amount of self-confidence—just the right amount—and this is courage. The courageous person is able and willing to take risks but also courageous enough to acknowledge his or her limits, thus avoiding excessive risk. Courage is a virtue. Moderation, for Aristotle, is the "golden mean" that defines virtue.

Applying this principle of moderation, Aristotle identified a number of virtues that a person whose life is guided by reason should possess. Just as courage is the virtuous middle point between cowardice and foolhardiness, so the virtue of pride lies between bashfulness and vanity. Realism is the virtuous middle point between pessimism and optimism, generosity, between stinginess and wastefulness, friendliness, between standoffishness and being overbearing, temperance, between self-denial and gluttony; modesty, between shame and shamelessness, justice, between callousness and wrath.

Aristotle's principle of moderation has been widely influential in moral philosophy and moral theology. Aside from its influence on professional theologians and philosophers,

Aristotle's application of the principle of moderation has an intrinsic, commonsense appeal. All of us have known people (perhaps ourselves) who have gotten into trouble by going overboard. The college student who gets into academic trouble because of too much partying and not enough studying would benefit from applying the principle of moderation. The workaholic who is emotionally unavailable to his family and who risks developing stress-related health problems would benefit from moderating his ambition. At the opposite end of the spectrum, those who lack initiative and fall short of what they should accomplish with their talents could also benefit from moderation. Indeed, we can fall into difficulty in life by doing too much or too little of almost anything.

Moderate Christians?

But, as practical as moderation may be, it seems to me an inappropriate term to describe our commitment to God. Claiming to be moderate in one's Christian faith is like saying, "Yes, I believe in Jesus, but not too strongly." Or, "Yes, I believe the Bible, but I try not to take it too seriously." A commitment to Christ isn't a moderate commitment. It isn't a partial or part-time commitment. It's an absolute commitment. God's love for us is immoderate. Christ's sacrifice for our sins was an immoderate sacrifice. We are called to respond with immoderate obedience and faithfulness. We are called to radical obedience.

As Generation X has ascended to media prominence, "extreme" has become a buzzword in American culture. We have extreme sports (accompanied, Madison Avenue tells us, by extreme thirst, which in turn requires an extreme sports drink), extreme travel, extreme adventure, extreme music, and extreme fashion. Extreme is also a good word for Christian discipleship. We can be extreme in our faith without being fundamentalist. That's what this book is about.

A Call to Extreme Faithfulness

In this book, I look to the message of the prophets of Israel to consider the way of life God's people are called to live. The prophets of Israel were often extreme individuals. Consider the ecstatic frenzies of Elijah and Elisha, the harsh pronouncements of Amos and Micah, the strange marriage of Hosea, or the wild symbolic antics of Jeremiah and Ezekiel. If those prophets were alive today, they just might be more at home among the purple-haired and body-pierced than among the staunch, stolid, well-groomed, churchgoing crowd. They were extreme in their commitment to the God who had called them, and they were extreme in presenting the message they had been given to proclaim.

Each of the prophets was a unique individual with a unique message for a particular community in a particular historical context. Yet it is possible to outline some common themes that make up what we might call the prophetic ethic. We can raise the question: what kind of life do the prophets call God's people to live?

The popular, conventional definition of a prophet is "someone who predicts the future." But the biblical prophets were primarily oriented toward the present. Scholars generally agree that the prophets' role was to call people to return to God's original demands as embodied in the Mosaic covenant. Over the years and generations, God's people turned aside from faithfulness to God's covenant. They allowed the wrong influences into their life together as a community. So God called out and sent prophets to call the community of Israel to repent and return to their first and true faith. The prophets condemned the injustice and unfaithfulness they saw around them, calling God's people to return in the here-and-now to the way of life God had outlined in the covenant with Moses at Mt. Sinai. God demands extreme faithfulness now!

The prophetic tradition of calling people to repent and live lives of extreme faithfulness echoes throughout the New Testament. John the Baptist appears in the desert decked out like a latter day Elijah, calling people to repent—to turn away from those influences that are leading them away from God. Jesus reveals a way of life in keeping with the true meaning and intent of God's covenant demands. Standing solidly in this prophetic tradition, Jesus calls people to repent of their unfaithfulness and injustice and turn to the way of life God intends for God's children. Paul echoes the prophetic tradition by exhorting the members of the churches to live in ways consistent with their status as children of God in Christ. When we talk about the message of the prophets, we're talking about an ethical tradition essential to New Testament Christianity.

Who Were the Prophets?

The practice of prophecy in the Ancient Near East probably had its origins in warfare. Before going into battle, a king or general would call upon a prophet to offer a sacrifice, perform some act of divination, and pronounce a curse on the enemy. We see this type of prophetic practice in the story of Balaam in Numbers 22-24. King Balak of Moab hires Balaam to pronounce a curse on the Israelites, but Balaam pronounces a blessing on Israel instead, much to King Balak's dismay. Even in this very primitive story, we see that Israel had a higher view of prophets than their neighbors. Prophets were not mere mercenaries, pronouncing blessings and curses for pay. A true prophet speaks only what God allows. The primary Hebrew term for prophet, *nabi*, means messenger or speaker. Another Hebrew term for prophets is *roeh*, which means seer. Prophets were often visionaries who put the visions they received from God into words as messages to God's people.

Within Israel, the prophets played a variety of roles. Moses is called a prophet, but he was also the political and administrative leader of Israel. Miriam, the sister of Moses, is also called a prophet when she leads a victory song after the miraculous crossing of the sea (see Exod. 15:4), as is Deborah the judge (Judg. 4:4), who, like Moses, was both prophet and chief administrator. In Samuel, we see the widest range of roles, including the primitive prophetic function of offering sacrifice before battle, priestly duties in the shrine at Shiloh, and the judges' offices of military and administrative leadership. In Samuel, we also see the development of a new role for prophets: anointing and advising kings.

Several prophets fulfilled this function of speaking truth to the powers by delivering messages of God's judgment to the king. Nathan confronted King David after David's rape/adultery with Bathsheba and subsequent murder of her husband Uriah (2 Sam. 12:1-15). Elijah pronounced God's judgment on King Ahab and his queen, Jezebel. Isaiah was a trusted advisor to Kings Ahaz and Hezekiah. Jeremiah's message of judgment was rejected by King Jehoiakim. Theologian Jorge Pixley suggests that the prophets' role with respect to the king was to remind the king that he served under a higher authority—that the king's power was not absolute. Peasant and king stood under the same covenant demands. In other words, the prophets served as a voice for the common people denying the king's right to oppress and abuse his subjects.

The prophets' role of speaking out against injustice and oppression is seen most clearly in the words of Amos and Micah, but also in the other prophets. At the end of the period of the judges, when the people first request a king, Samuel warns them that their kings will oppress them (1 Sam. 8:10-18). When Nathan confronts King David after the Bathsheba affair, he does so with a parable about a rich man who abuses a poor neighbor. Similarly, Elijah's indictment against Ahab and Jezebel after their seizure of Naboth's vineyard is an indictment of the royal family's abuse of power (1 Kings 21). God demands that the poor be treated with justice, fairness, and compassion.

Extreme Virtues

I have chosen to outline the prophetic ethic in terms of virtues—extreme virtues. Virtues are character traits—good habits, or steady dispositions to behave in certain ways. A person who possesses the right cluster of virtues is said to have good character. Most approaches to ethics focus either on rules and principles that should guide decisions and actions, or on calculating which course of action among the available options will bring about the best outcome for everyone concerned. Virtue ethics, also called character ethics, focuses instead on the character that people or communities develop and show over a lifetime. As we've seen, Aristotle outlined the virtues by applying the principle of moderation to the various spheres of human activity.

In the middle of the twentieth century, G .E. M. Anscombe called for a revival of an Aristotelian approach to ethics. She suggested that we can think of virtues the way we think about intelligence: everyone has a virtue quotient, or VQ. Most people would fall within the normal range on the virtue scale. Those who possess a large quantity of virtue would be moral geniuses, or saints. At the lower end of the scale we would find psychopaths, criminals, and other moral degenerates. More recently, theorists such as philosopher Alisdair MacIntyre and Christian ethicist Stanley Hauerwas have suggested that virtues are tied to the needs of life in community, or to the social practices of the various professions and vocations necessary for a society to thrive.

Aristotle and others have taught that virtue is learned by habit. The extreme virtues I'm advocating here can also be learned by habit. We develop the kind of character God calls us to by having our imaginations shaped by the story of God's self-revelation in Scripture and by becoming part of the story of God's people. Developing habits requires effort. Prayer, Bible study, self-examination, reflection, and participation in a community of faith where we experience mutual accountability for our discipleship are essential, daily ingredients in developing virtuous character.

The extreme virtues we discover and learn in Scripture combine to form a portrait of the kind of character God's people should exhibit as individuals and in our life together. The virtues I explore in the following chapters are not an exhaustive list. Nor do I attempt any systematic treatment of the prophets and their message(s). What I offer are prayerful meditations for persons who, like me, struggle to have our character shaped by God's Word as we move into the third millennium.

Being God's people in a postmodern age is an extreme challenge that calls for extreme commitment. Journey with me into the world of the prophets and the extreme virtues they advocate and embody.

READ: ISAIAH 58:1-12

What to me is the multitude of your sacrifices?
says the LORD;
I have had enough of burnt offerings of rams
and the fat of fed beasts;
I do not delight in the blood of bulls, or of
lambs, or of goats.
—Isaiah 1:11

I appeal to you therefore, brothers and sisters, by
the mercies of God, to present your bodies as a
living sacrifice, holy and acceptable to God,
which is your spiritual worship.
—Romans 12:1

one

SACRIFICE

after the horrific events of September 11, 2001, an idea that had been in decline in our society re-emerged as a heroic ideal: the idea of sacrifice. Firefighters, police officers, and even ordinary citizens became heroes by risking and, tragically for many, losing their lives to save others. In the subsequent weeks and months, appeals were made for the rest of us to be willing to sacrifice some of our freedoms for the sake of national security.

Sacrifice, of course, is not a new idea. For many generations, the ideal of sacrifice held an honored place in our culture's pantheon of values. As late as the turbulent 1960s, the decade often pointed at by conservative critics as the fountainhead of our nation's moral decline, President John F. Kennedy was able to inspire a generation with the challenge, "Ask not what your country can do for you; ask what you can do for your country." Earlier generations learned about sacrifice and associated sacrifice with heroism. There was a time, before the era of eight-figure salaries, when athletes could become heroes by sacrificing individual glory for the sake of their teams. Soldiers became heroes by being willing to sacrifice themselves for their nation and its ideals. Civil rights marchers exhibited heroism by putting themselves in harm's way for the sake of freedom and equality. Parents still become heroes through the thousand small sacrifices they make day by day for their children.

But the 1980s was the decade of "conspicuous consumption." A culture of consumerism grew, in which advertisements and popular media, along with easy credit, promoted an ethic of instant self-gratification. Then the 1990s saw the stock markets engage in a wild orgy of wealth-creation primarily through grossly over-valued technology companies. The growing culture of consumerism had all but erased sacrifice from our public lexicon. Politicians no longer appealed to voters' sense of self-sacrifice, but encouraged instead a sense of entitlement and self-indulgence.

After the bursting of the technology bubble, financial malfeasance in a variety of industries has been publicized through a number of high-profile scandals. The economic decline that has unfolded in these same months has forced involuntary sacrifices upon many. Ironically, alongside appeals to sacrifice our freedoms for the sake of national security, appeals have been made for citizens to revive their exuberant spending habits in order to revive the nation's economy. Apparently, in our topsy-turvy world, self-sacrifice and self-indulgence go hand in hand. We can give away our cake and eat it too! But through all the advances and recessions in the dominant cultural mood—from the exuberant consumerism of the 1980s and 1990s to the more reflective mood following September 11—stories of sacrifice have had the power to inspire.

The language of sacrifice also occupies a large place in the Christian faith. Throughout Scripture, we read about sacrifice. The Old Testament tells of sacrifices by the priests for the sins of the people. The New Testament tells of Jesus becoming our high priest and the complete sacrifice for our sins. And we, as God's people in Christ, are called to live sacrificially—to become a "living sacrifice" (Rom. 12:1). What does all this talk about sacrifice really mean?

If we were to reconstruct the history of the human religious quest, we would find that the most primitive understandings of sacrifice were simplistic. The underlying assumption was that the gods had needs like human needs. The gods needed food. Meat and grain offered as sacrifices were given because the gods were hungry. People expected that the gods would be grateful for the gifts and would respond by sending favorable weather, or by removing disease, or by performing whatever else the human supplicants desired. Such religion aimed at meeting the needs of the gods to bend the will of the gods to suit human purposes.

Biblical religion is diametrically opposed to such an approach. In biblical religion, sacrifice is designed neither to meet God's needs nor to bend God's will toward human purposes. Instead, sacrifice becomes an act of giving something we value to God as a symbol of our willingness to make our whole lives and all our resources available to God. In biblical religion, sacrifice doesn't seek to make God do what we want. Instead, it shows that God's people are willing to do what God wants.

These two distinct ways to approach God are sometimes designated magic and faith. Magic is the self-centered effort to manipulate God (or the gods) for human purposes; faith is the self-sacrificial willingness to make our lives available to God for God's purposes. Unfortunately, God's people in Scripture sometimes failed to uphold the distinction and let their sacrifices and other religious acts become efforts at magical manipulation rather than symbolic expressions of sacrificial faith.

Isaiah 58 offers a good case study of God's rejection of self-centered, manipulative religious devotion. Here, the prophet answers the complaints of the people, first repeating their question to God: "Why do we fast, but you do not see? Why humble ourselves, but you do not notice?" (Isa. 58:3). The situation is the travail and hardship of the post-exilic period. After years in far away Babylon, a group of exiles had returned home to rebuild the temple in Jerusalem and re-establish their life in the Promised Land. But times are difficult. Work is hard, food is in short supply, and hostility exists between the returned exiles and their new neighbors.

They declared and observed a fast, but the expected blessing from God has not come. They want to know why God refuses to honor their efforts when they have followed the set guidelines for fasting. The prophet's answer is that God has greater concerns than correctly performed ritual. Their worship is not pleasing to God because their worship is empty. Their fasting isn't an expression of their desire to serve God; rather, their fast is self-serving. "Look," the prophet responds, "you serve your own interest on your fast day, and oppress all your workers. Look, you fast only to quarrel and to fight and to strike with a wicked fist. Such fasting as you do today will not make your voice heard on high" (Isa. 58:3-4).

God has no interest in religious practice that masks violence, greed, and other defects of character. To be pleasing to God, worship must be accompanied by ethical living. In fact, ethical living *is* the worship God desires.

> Is not this the fast that I choose:
>   to loose the bonds of injustice,
>   to undo the thongs of the yoke,
> to let the oppressed go free,
>   and to break every yoke?
> Is it not to share your bread with the hungry,
>   and bring the homeless poor into your house;

when you see the naked, to cover them,
    and not to hide yourself from your own kin?
    (Isa. 58:6-7)

The kind of worship that pleases God consists of justice for the oppressed, food for the hungry, shelter for the homeless, clothing for the naked. What is important to God is the way we treat people in our day-to-day relationships: our personal relationships, our business relationships, our economic relationships, our political relationships, *all* our relationships. Among God's people, sacrifice is a symbol of one's willingness to make one's life and one's resources available to God and to one's neighbor in God's name.

The prophets repeatedly remind us that sacrifices and other acts of religious devotion are not recipes for receiving God's blessings. God is, in fact, quite displeased when sacrifice loses its character as a symbolic act of faithful commitment and becomes an act of selfish manipulation. Isaiah announces, "What to me is the multitude of your sacrifices? says the LORD; I have had enough of bunt offerings of rams" (Isa. 1:11). Jeremiah follows suit: "Of what use to me is frankincense that comes from Sheba, or sweet cane from a distant land? Your burnt offerings are not acceptable, nor are your sacrifices pleasing to me" (Jer. 6:20). Hosea sums up God's priorities: "For I desire steadfast love and not sacrifice, the knowledge of God rather than burnt offerings" (Hos. 6:6). God desires that a sacrificial spirit be consistently evident in the ways we relate to God and to one another.

God is less concerned with what we do when we come to formal worship than with what we do in our daily lives. God wants our daily lives to show the spirit of sacrifice, that willingness to make our whole life and all our resources available to God and God's children. Sacrifice per se, of course, is not part of Christian worship. The closest we come, perhaps, is the giving of offerings. In bringing an offering to God, we bring a token of our gratitude that symbolizes our willingness to put our whole self at God's disposal. And if we do not give our offerings in such a spirit of sacrifice, then God is no more pleased with us than with the empty worship the prophets condemned so many years ago.

When Hosea proclaims that God desires mercy, or "steadfast love," rather than sacrifice, he is not setting up an either/or dichotomy. Steadfast love embodied in day-to-day relationships *is* the sacrifice God demands. This is the aim of Paul's exhortation in Romans 12:1: "present your bodies as a living sacrifice." Our very lives are our sacrifice to God. We are to live sacrificially. Every moment of every day belongs not to us, but to God. Paul exhorts further: "Do not be conformed to this world, but be transformed by the renewing of your minds" (Rom. 12:2). To be a living sacrifice means being transformed rather than conformed—not seeking to bend God's will to suit our purposes, but seeking to have our mind and our will transformed so we are in tune with God's purposes. To be a living sacrifice is to be, as Martin Luther King Jr., put it, a "transformed nonconformist."

In the following chapters, we consider several virtues that the biblical prophets called God's people to. In admonishing the people to return to faithful adherence to the demands of their covenant relationship with God, the prophets call for consistency between words spoken in worship and deeds done in daily relationships. Integrity is another word for this. To practice integrity as members of God's people, we must be willing to live sacrificially, to make our lives our sacrifice to God. To be a living sacrifice means that every minute of our lives belongs to God and that all our resources are available to God.

In our society, sacrifice is a particularly extreme idea. Everything around us encourages self-indulgence rather than self-sacrifice. Our economy depends upon our willingness to dole out buckets of money to indulge ourselves and our families in luxury items and leisure pursuits. Advertisers as well as politicians are quick to reinforce the idea that we are absolutely entitled to indulge ourselves in this way. Popular psychology teaches us to take care of ourselves, if need be at the expense of what some might consider obligations to others. Much of what passes for religion or spirituality in our society also carries this message of self-indulgence. Many expressions of "New Age" spirituality, for example, promise improvements in one's well-being at little or no personal cost. The appeal is to our desire for self-improvement. The biblical call to sacrifice, however, is a call to self-denial.

Churches often reinforce the culture of self-indulgence. People shop around for the church that best meets their felt needs, so we have "seeker-sensitive" services designed to be more appealing and less demanding to those who aren't sure they want to take on any of the obligations associated with religious practice. But even some of the older, more traditional practices can implicitly work against the grain of the biblical call to sacrificial living. For example, doesn't old-fashioned, revivalistic evangelism, with its exhortation to avoid eternal punishment and gain eternal rewards, represent an appeal to our self-interest?

The Christian gospel teaches that God in Christ has made an extreme sacrifice to save us from our sinfulness, and it calls on God's people to practice the extreme virtue of sacrificial living. In the fourth beatitude in the Sermon on the Mount, Jesus declares, "Blessed are those who hunger and thirst for righteousness, for they will be filled" (Matt. 5:6). To live sacrificially means to hunger and thirst for righteousness, for God's way of being in the world. To live sacrificially means our desire to live as God wants us to is our strongest, perhaps our only, desire. To live sacrificially means that we spend every minute of our lives desiring God and that, in every relationship, we treat other people as children of God.

So let us resolve to live sacrificially, following Christ who withheld nothing in living and dying sacrificially for our sake. Let us put our whole selves at God's disposal, so God can shape our character after the model of extreme virtue proclaimed by the prophets and exhibited by Jesus. Let us make all our resources available to God, so that we embody extreme virtues in our relationships with others. And let us do so not for the sake of rewards, but simply because we have experienced and are responding to the claim of God on our lives.

For Reflection and Action

1. Pay attention to the messages you receive from television and other media. How many times a day do you receive the message that you are entitled to self-indulgence? How does this message of self-indulgence affect your ability to develop a spirit of self-sacrifice as part of your character?

2. Think of people you have known or known of who have made sacrifices that you admire. What motivated their sacrifice? How can you make a similar sacrifice?

3. Read Philippians 2:1-11 and reflect prayerfully on the self-emptying sacrifice made by Christ. Pray that the sacrificial mind of Christ will become yours.

Prayer

God,
Our Ruler and Redeemer,
Giver of all good gifts,
We thank you for the talents and resources you have
given us,

And for the opportunities and challenges you have
    placed in our path.
Make us good stewards of every talent, every resource,
    and every opportunity.
Free us from the temptations of self-indulgence,
And put in us a desire to live sacrificially,
After the example of and for the sake of
Jesus Christ, our Lord.
Amen.

READ: AMOS 1:1—3:2

You only have I known of all the families
of the earth; therefore I will punish you
for all your iniquities.
—*Amos 3:2*

two

RESPONSIBILITY

The prophet Amos announces a rather unsettling promise. Amos is a prophet from the southern kingdom, Judah, sent by God to address the sins of the northern kingdom, Israel. He comes to the king's sanctuary at Bethel, where the congregation would naturally be unreceptive to his message. After all, he is from across the border, and there is much resentment in the northern kingdom toward the religious elitism down south. So Amos devises a clever strategy. He wins his audience's ear by pronouncing God's judgment on their enemies. One by one, Amos describes the sins by which Israel's enemies have incurred God's wrath. We can imagine the congregation shouting "Amen!" as Amos describes God's displeasure with the Syrians, the Philistines, the Phoenicians, the Edomites, the Ammonites, and the Moabites (Amos 1:3–2:3). And when Amos pronounces God's judgment on even his own home country, Judah, the "Amens!" reach a crescendo (Amos 2:4-5).

But Amos is not a seeker-sensitive preacher. He's not interested in leaving his congregation feeling good about themselves. He carries the message to its logical and necessary conclusion: if God is displeased with all these other nations for their sins, how much more is God displeased with the sins of Israel! And if God's judgment is coming to all these other nations, God's judgment is surely coming to Israel as well (Amos 2:6-8).

Israel—especially Israel—cannot avoid responsibility for transgressing God's demands. "You only have I known of all the families of the earth; therefore I will punish you for all your iniquities" (Amos 3:2).

Jesus pronounces this same basic principle of responsibility in Luke 12:48: "To whom much has been given, much will be required." In other words, God's people are expected to live up to what God has entrusted us with. We have been given the blessing of salvation and so many other blessings! We are responsible for how we live out our salvation. We are responsible for how we receive and use all of the blessings God gives us. In *The Responsible Self*, theologian H. Richard Niebuhr describes the Christian life in terms of an ethic of responsibility. "God is acting in all actions upon you," Niebuhr says. Our task is to discern what God is doing in our lives and our surroundings, and to carry out a fitting response to God's action. By the way we live our lives, we are writing the story of our own discipleship. We are responsible for how that story turns out.

Many social critics note that our society has (d)evolved to the point where calls for responsibility are barely understood, let alone heeded. In *The Spirit of Community*, Amitai Etzioni cites many indicators of the diminished repute of responsibility in American society. According to one study Etzioni cites, an overwhelming majority of young adults believe they have a *right* to be tried before a jury of their peers if they are ever accused of a crime, yet only a small fraction of those surveyed felt they had a *responsibility* to serve on a jury if called. As a society, we've lost sight of the inexorable fact that *no* rights exist without accompanying responsibilities.

But is the failure to take responsibility for our actions really new? The Bible presents a connection between human sinfulness and the refusal to take responsibility for our own actions from the very start. Remember the story of Adam and Eve in the garden of Eden? After transgressing God's command not to eat of the tree in the middle of the garden, Adam and Eve try to hide from God. God confronts Adam: "Have you eaten of the tree of which I commanded you not to eat?" (Gen. 3:11). Adam replies, "The *woman* whom *you* gave to be with me, she gave me fruit from the tree, and I ate" (3:12, italics added). Note Adam's double evasion of responsibility here: the *woman* is to blame first and foremost, and *God* is to blame for having made the woman. God turns to the woman next: "What is this that you have done?" She too tries to pass the responsibility onto someone else: "The *serpent* tricked me, and I ate" (3:13). God does not give the serpent an opportunity to evade responsibility. And, of course, with the ensuing curse, God holds all parties responsible for their wrongdoing.

We find another biblical example of evasion of responsibility in the story of the Israelites at Mount Sinai. While Moses is on the mountain communing with God, the people grow impatient. They say to Aaron, "Come, make gods for us, who shall go before us; as for this Moses, ... we do not know what has become of him" (Exod. 32:1). Aaron asks the people to gather their gold jewelry and bring it to him. Then Aaron "took the gold from them, formed it in a mold, and cast an image of a calf" (32:4). The story is quite clear in describing Aaron's creation of the golden calf as an intentional act. Later, after Moses has returned and angrily destroyed not only the idol but also the stone tablets on which God had inscribed the Ten Commandments, Moses confronts Aaron: "What did this people do to you that you have brought so great a sin upon them?" (32:21). Aaron tells

Moses about the people's impatience and their request that Aaron make gods for them. Then Aaron describes his own role in the process: "So I said to them, 'Whoever has gold, take it off'; so they gave it to me, and I threw it into the fire, and out came this calf!" (32:24). As if it had been an accident! When confronted with his wrongdoing, Aaron refuses to take responsibility.

Adam, Eve, and Aaron aren't unique. They exemplify the biblical portrait of the human condition. There's just something not quite right about human nature. We often act irresponsibly—even downright badly at times. Then, when confronted with what we've done, we still don't want to take responsibility. This is part of what theologians mean by original sin: some basic flaw in human character prevents us from being all that God created us to be. The good news is that God by grace accepts us as we are and by the Holy Spirit empowers us in the process of becoming the people God intends us to be. Though the initiative and the power in the process of salvation belong to God, the responsibility remains ours. We must respond to God's initiative. We must respond to God's acting in all actions upon us. And as we grow toward being the people God created us to be, we grow in responsibility. The responsibility God calls us to has several dimensions.

First, we are responsible for our own sinfulness. This is basic to the teaching of Amos and the other prophets. As we have seen, Amos begins by pointing out the sins of Israel's enemies. This is an easy message to receive—all of us know what's wrong with the people we don't like. But when Amos points out the logical conclusion that if God is punishing the other nations for their sins, then God will also punish Israel for many of the same sins, his audience turns against him. The words of Jesus apply here: "Do not judge, so that you may not be judged. For with the judgment you make you will be judged, and the measure you give will be the measure you get" (Matt. 7:1-2).

The message for us is simple: we are responsible for our own sin. Regardless of what other people do, we are responsible for our own sin. Even if everyone else is doing it, we are responsible for our own sin. Even if others do it and get away with it, we are responsible for our own sin. (Speaking of which, I've never quite understood how so many people get away with driving too fast all the time, while I get caught on those rare occasions when I do exceed the speed limit!) Even if others provoke us and make us mad, we are responsible for our own sin. No matter what anyone else does, each of us is responsible before God for our own sin. We are to repent, which means to stop committing that sin, turn away from it and not do it again, and return to the way of living God lays out for us in the teachings of Scripture.

Second, we are responsible to our neighbors. We've seen how Adam and Eve and Aaron refused to take responsibility for their sin when confronted by God. Another person near the beginning of the biblical story was confronted by God for his sin, whose reply teaches us another lesson about responsibility. I am referring to the story of Cain, who murdered his brother Abel. After the heinous crime, God says to Cain, "Where is your brother Abel?" Cain replies, "I do not know; am I my brother's keeper?" (Gen. 4:9). The implied answer is, Yes, we are our brother's keeper and our sister's keeper. We are our neighbor's keeper.

We are responsible to our neighbors—not for our neighbors' sin, but for doing what we can to ensure our neighbors' well-being. The specific sins Amos and the other prophets most often condemn are sins related to the failure to take adequate responsibility for weaker members of the community. "Thus says the LORD: For three transgressions of Israel, and for four, I will not revoke the punishment; because they sell the righteous for silver, and the needy for a pair of san-dals—they who trample the head of the poor into the dust of the earth, and push the afflicted out of the way" (Amos 2:6-7). Further,

> Therefore, because you trample on the poor
>> and take from them levies of grain,
> you have built houses of hewn stone,
>> but you shall not live in them;
> you have planted pleasant vineyards,
>> but you shall not drink their wine.
> For I know how many are your transgressions,
>> and how great are your sins—
> you who afflict the righteous, who take a bribe,
>> and push aside the needy in the gate
>> (Amos 5:11-12).

Protection for the poor, the weak, and the stranger was built into God's law from the outset. Deuteronomy 10:17-19, for example, expresses a sentiment found throughout the Law of Moses:

> For the LORD your God is God of gods and Lord of lords, the great God, mighty and awesome, who is not partial and takes no bribe, who executes justice for the orphan and the widow, and who loves the strangers, providing them food and clothing. You shall also love the stranger, for you were strangers in the land of Egypt.

The Torah, or Law, clearly presents responsibility for the poor as a requirement grounded in the very character of God. The failure to observe basic justice for the poor, says Amos, is now going to result in judgment and destruction. We *are* our neighbor's keeper.

During the New Testament era, Christians had gotten the message that we are responsible for our neighbor's well-being to the extent that Paul could exhort the Thessalonians, with respect to their love for one another, "just as you are doing, you do so more and more" (1 Thess. 4:1, RSV). If you are part of a loving congregation that takes seriously the biblical mandate of responsibility for our neighbors—especially the weaker members of society—then I offer you the same advice Paul gave the Thessalonians: "Just as you are doing, you do so more and more."

But we live in a culture of individualism where most Christians tend to see the Christian faith as a private matter between an individual and God with no implications for social relationships. And we live in a culture of consumerism and narcissism where churches adopt marketing practices and individuals grow accustomed to thinking in terms of what they can receive from their faith rather than what it might require of them. And we live in a culture of callousness and violence where we must be vigilant not to forget that Jesus' command is to love all our neighbors—even our enemies! Baptist ethicist Henlee Barnett has defined the kind of love Jesus commands as "to will and to work for the well-being of others." We are our neighbor's keeper.

Third, we are responsible for our stewardship of our resources. In Amos' view, this makes Israel's situation unique: "You only have I known of all the families of the earth; therefore I will punish you for all your iniquities." Israel was God's special nation, God's covenant partner, the recipient of God's law and God's blessings. Israel was expected to be a faithful covenant partner, to be obedient to God's law. "To whom much has been given, much will be required." Christians are the recipients of God's salvation, of God's grace and forgiveness. We are expected to imitate and model that grace and forgiveness in our relationships. We are expected to live lives of holiness and faithfulness, even in midst of a perverse generation in a fallen and sinful world.

While I was a doctoral student at Southern Baptist Theological Seminary, Emilio Castro, then General Secretary of the World Council of Churches, came to deliver the annual Gheens Lectures. During his visit to campus, he addressed a luncheon gathering of doctoral students, reminding us of some stark, statistical realities. Less than half of the world's population learns to read and write. Less than one percent of the world's population ever attends a college or university. Yet here we were blessed with opportunity to pursue education all the way to the Ph.D. level. He challenged us to ask ourselves "Why?" and "Why me?" and to remember Jesus' challenge, "To whom much has been given, much will be required." Education is a great blessing, and all blessings carry with them responsibilities. We were challenged to show our gratitude by finding ways to use our education for the benefit of others.

I share these statistics with my own students, who are, after all, part of that less than one percent of the world's population who have the opportunity to attend a college or university. I want them to hear the challenge: "To whom much has been given, much will be required." I want them to think about their responsibility to take their education more seriously and to use their education for the benefit of others. They look at me like I'm crazy. This is America, after all. College is part of their entitlement. They take college for granted. It's their gateway to the high-paying job that will bring them all the personal luxuries they've ever wanted. What do you mean responsibility? The message of the gospel is that, even in America, we are responsible to recognize the blessings God gives us and use them for the sake of God and God's children.

Finally, we are responsible for how we relate to God. If God is acting in all actions upon us, then all our responses are responses to God's action. Let's turn our attention from Amos to another prophet who prophesied during the same period of Israel's history, Hosea. Hosea looks at the same situation Amos addressed and sees the basic problem as Israel's unfaithfulness. Using his own marriage to an unfaithful woman as an example, Hosea portrays Israel as an unfaithful wife who has turned away from her husband and "played the whore" by pursuing other lovers. God's message comes through Hosea: "She did not know that it was I who gave her the grain, the wine, and the oil, and who lavished upon her silver and gold that they used for Baal" (Hos. 2:8). Israel had taken the blessings of God and acted as if those blessings had come from somewhere else. Israel believed falsely that participation in the Canaanite fertility cult was what had brought them fruitful harvests and prosperity. They had received the blessings of God and responded by thanking someone else.

Isn't that the condition of so many people today? We enjoy the advantages of so many wonderful things that God has enabled us to enjoy. God, after all, is the author of all human abilities and therefore the ultimate source of all human accomplishments. Yet most people take all these things for granted. Most people act as if all the things we have were gotten without God's help. We show no gratitude; we act as if God doesn't matter at all.

Amos says God is coming in judgment. Hosea agrees, but says that the judgment is not the end. The coming judgment, Hosea says, will pave the way for a new beginning.

> Therefore, I will now allure her,
>> and bring her into the wilderness,
>> and speak tenderly to her....
> There she shall respond as in the days of her youth,
>> as at the time when she came out of the land of
>> Egypt (Hos. 2:14-15).

The coming judgment is so that Israel will wake up, turn around, return, and be faithful once again to the Lord. Judgment is to open the door to grace. The New Testament message is that Jesus Christ has taken upon himself the judgment for our sin. So our task is to respond to God's grace with simple gratitude to God for what God has done in forgiving our sins, in empowering us by the Holy Spirit to live a meaningful and abundant life, in giving us means to provide for our basic needs. God is acting in all actions upon us. Our task, every day, every moment, is to discern what God is doing in our lives and our surroundings, and to respond with appropriate measure of gratitude and with conviction and action that move us closer to being the people God intends us to be.

This is responsibility—our fitting response to God in each moment of our lives.

For Reflection and Action

1. Reflect on the implications of these statements:
   a. I am responsible for my own spiritual development.
   b. I am responsible for becoming the person God intends me to be.
   c. I am responsible for helping my neighbor when I can.
   d. I am responsible for serving God through the ministries of my church.

   What are you doing to fulfill these responsibilities? What do you need to do to fulfill these responsibilities more effectively?

2. Reflect further on Jesus' challenge, "To whom much has been given, much will be required." What have you been given and what are those blessings requiring of you?

Prayer

God,
Our Author and Creator,
You have made us in your image
And created us for your purposes.
But our lives often fail to reflect your image clearly,
So we fail to fulfill your purposes completely.
Forgive us our shortcomings,
And give us the wisdom and the strength
To fulfill the responsibilities you have established for us
And to become the people you intend us to be.
Amen.

READ: AMOS 4:1—5:24

But let justice roll down like waters,
and righteousness like an ever-flowing stream.
—Amos 5:24

People are bowed down, everyone is brought low,
and the eyes of the haughty are humbled.
But the LORD of hosts is exalted by justice,
and the Holy God shows himself holy
by righteousness.
—Isaiah 5:15-16

three

JUSTICE

Justice is the central ethical demand of the prophets. Amos's words—"Let justice roll down like waters"—echo like a clarion call across the years, calling God's people in all times and places to work so justice will prevail in human societies. But what do the prophets mean by justice?

It is easy for modern Americans to miss the centrality of the ethical demand of justice in the Bible. Most of us grew up with the King James Version of the Bible, where the Hebrew word *mishpat* is usually rendered as judgment rather than justice. Moreover, we have come to interpret the word righteousness, *tsedaqah*, as a form of private piety when, in fact, righteousness is a synonym for justice! Baptist ethicist Glen Stassen counts 1,060 references to justice in Scripture. So why don't we hear more about justice from our pulpits and from popular Christian leaders? Why, when some radical declares that justice is the central ethical demand of Scripture, are we surprised? Given that the Bible contains no mention at all of abortion and only eight possible references to homosexual acts, one wonders where American Christianity is getting its ethical priorities.

And yet, even if we accept that justice is central to biblical ethics, we are still at high risk of misunderstanding biblical justice. Biblical justice is not what modern Americans usually think of as justice. When we hear the word justice, we most likely think of criminal justice, which deals in retributive justice. On many college and university campuses, including some at which I've taught, Criminal Justice is the fastest growing major. I am somewhat troubled to know that I live in a society where criminology is among the major growth industries. So I can understand that in a society so preoccupied with crime, the most prevalent meaning of justice would be retributive justice. But, while a portion of the biblical texts do deal with issues of crime and punishment, retributive justice is not the focus of biblical justice.

Another type of justice is distributive justice, which is concerned with the way the things that make up the good life are distributed among individuals and groups within society. Distributive justice is much closer to what the Bible has in view when it talks about justice. But even if we recognize that justice is central to biblical ethics, and that biblical justice is more distributive than retributive, more social than criminal, we have not eliminated the risk of missing the meaning of biblical justice. In our society, we tend to assume that the market economy will automatically distribute society's goods justly. In other words, we tend to reduce distributive justice to procedural justice. As long as procedures and transactions are fair and honest, we assume justice is served. Everyone receives what his or her talents and initiative can earn in the free market—this is right and just in our eyes. We also tend to assume that religion is mostly a private matter between an individual and God. Religion, we think, has little place in the public arena, and it certainly makes no demands on social institutions or economic relationships.

The Bible makes no such assumption. The prophets were fully aware that the prosperous could exploit the underprivileged and marginalized, and they roundly condemned such exploitation. The prophets mention the need for fair procedures, such as honest weights and measures (Mic. 6:11). But procedural justice is the minimum framework of justice, not its maximum obligation. Just outcomes, not merely just procedures, are the test of biblical justice. Biblical justice is not merely distributive; it is restorative. Biblical justice aims at restoring the marginalized to full participation in the community.

The prophets didn't believe that religious devotion could be separated from socio-economic realities. They proclaim that God rejects the worship of those who willingly spread and take part in unjust social structures and economic systems. Biblical justice means compassion toward the poor and full inclusion of all members in the community. As we saw in our discussion of sacrifice, biblical faith must get worked out in all our relationships, including our political and economic relationships.

Let's look at some examples. Amos describes Israel's systematic injustice toward the poor:

> Therefore because you trample on the poor
>   and take from them levies of grain,
> you have built houses of hewn stone,
>   but you shall not live in them;
> you have planted pleasant vineyards,
>   but you shall not drink their wine.
> For I know how many are your transgressions,
>   and how great are your sins—
> you who afflict the righteous, who take a bribe,
>   and push aside the needy in the gate (Amos 5:11-12).

Because of these injustices, God no longer accepts Israel's worship. In fact, injustice has made their worship an annoyance to God.

I hate, I despise your festivals,
    and I take no delight in your solemn assemblies.
Even though you offer me your burnt offerings and
        grain offerings,
    I will not accept them;
and the offerings of well-being of your fatted animals,
    I will not look upon.
Take away from me the noise of your songs;
    I will not listen to the melody of your harps.
But let justice roll down like waters,
    and righteousness like an ever-flowing stream
    (Amos 5:21-24).

Amos proclaims that God demands justice in daily dealings, not piety in weekly worship.

In Micah, we find a similar situation in which injustice has rendered worship invalid. Micah presents a courtroom-style dialogue in which the people question why God is not pleased with their worship. The people complain:

With what shall I come before the LORD,
    and bow myself before God on high?
Shall I come before him with burnt offerings,
    with calves a year old?
Will the LORD be pleased with thousands of rams,
    with ten thousand rivers of oil?
Shall I give my firstborn for my transgression,
    the fruit of my body for the sin of my soul? (Mic. 6:6-7)

Here the people sarcastically imply that God's demands are too stringent and too difficult to discern. No, the prophet replies, God's demands are simple and well-known:

> He has told you, O mortal, what is good;
>> and what does the LORD require of you
> but to do justice, and to love kindness,
>> and to walk humbly with your God? (Mic. 6:8)

Like Amos, Micah makes clear that what God demands is daily justice rather than the motions of proper religious ritual.

As we saw in chapter 1, a similar episode occurs in Isaiah 58. A fast has been declared and observed, yet God has not rewarded the fasters with the blessing they expected. They want to know why God does not respond to their properly observed ritual of fasting. "Why do we fast, but you do not see?" they ask. "Why humble ourselves, but you do not notice?" (Isa. 58:3). The prophet answers: "Look, you serve your own interest on your fast day, and oppress all your workers" (Isa. 58:3). The prophet elaborates, declaring again that daily justice as compassion for the poor is the service God demands. The message is clear. Time and time again the prophets proclaim that God demands justice, that oppression and exploitation of the poor and marginalized come to an end, and that these people be treated as full and equal members of the community.

This same demand for justice as compassion for the poor carries over into the New Testament era. Echoing Amos and Micah, Jesus pronounces blessings on the poor and curses on the wealthy:

> Blessed are you who are poor,
>> for yours is the kingdom of God.
> Blessed are you who are hungry now,
>> for you will be filled.
> Blessed are you who weep now,
>> for you will laugh....
> But woe to you who are rich,

for you have received your consolation.
Woe to you who are full now,
    for you will be hungry.
Woe to you who are laughing now,
    for you will mourn and weep (Luke 6:20-21, 24-25).

Mary, the mother of Jesus, also prophesies the inversion of the status of the rich and poor: "[God] has filled the hungry with good things, and sent the rich away empty" (Luke 1:53). James echoes the teaching of Jesus: "Listen, my beloved brothers and sisters. Has not God chosen the poor in the world to be rich in faith and to be heirs of the kingdom that he has promised to those who love him?" (2:5). The biblical witness is clear: God is on the side of the poor! Justice is God's demand on behalf of the poor.

So far, we've been examining justice as a demand—as an ethical principle—but what does it mean to claim that justice is a virtue—an extreme virtue—that God's people should develop and embody in the way we live? For indeed, biblical justice is more than an abstract principle or ideal. Biblical scholar Walther Zimmerli contrasts the abstract, philosophical understanding of justice—symbolized by a blind scale—with the biblical view: "Justice in the Old Testament is never blind *Justitia*. It is always understood as part of open-eyed compassion." Abraham Joshua Heschel notes the dynamic character of biblical justice: "Justice is not a mere norm, but a fighting challenge, a restless drive." Biblical justice is a raging river (Amos 5:24), a force waiting to burst into concrete reality and overflow through God's people into a world awash with injustice. How do we make this force a reality in our lives? How can we live out the extreme virtue of justice in an unjust world?

The first step is to appreciate the justice of God. I quoted above Luke's version of Jesus' Beatitudes. Most of us are more familiar with Matthew's version, where Jesus begins his Sermon on the Mount by pronouncing, "Blessed are the poor in spirit, for theirs is the kingdom of heaven" (Matt. 5:3). To appreciate the justice of God, we must acknowledge our own spiritual poverty. We are spiritually destitute. We possess nothing with which we can make ourselves presentable to God. We fail to love God with our whole being, and we fail to love our neighbor as ourselves. The human condition is that we are sinners, utterly impoverished before God, and possessing no means by which to justify ourselves. So God provides a means for our justification—this is the message of the gospel. What we cannot provide for ourselves, God provides for us. God is just and God's justice means compassion for poor sinners.

When we appreciate God's justice in light of our own spiritual poverty, we come to realize that everything we have stems from God's compassion—that we have not earned any of the things God has blessed us with. Our talents, our opportunities, our material resources, our loved ones—all are gifts of God. Therefore, none of these things presents a basis for thinking of ourselves more highly than we think of others. This is another aspect of our spiritual poverty: before an infinitely good God, all sinners are equally impoverished. All children of dust are equally children of God. All are equally deserving of justice. As Isaiah declares:

> People are bowed down, everyone is brought low,
>   and the eyes of the haughty are humbled.
> But the LORD of hosts is exalted by justice
>   and the Holy God shows himself holy by righteousness (Isa. 5:15-16).

Before God's justice, we are humbled. If we "do justice"—if justice forms our character—then we will indeed "walk humbly" with God (Mic. 6:8).

Justice, like steadfast love, is rooted in the character of God. In fact, justice and steadfast love are closely related. Granted, there are times in Scripture when God's compassionate justice gives way to God's righteous judgment. Basically, the sins upon which the prophets declare God's judgment fall into two categories. The first of these, injustice toward the poor, has been a focus of this chapter. The second is idolatry or unfaithfulness, taking the devotion that belongs to God and offering it to someone or something else. Both sins have in common the failure to acknowledge God as who God is, which is also a failure to acknowledge our true standing before God. Injustice and idolatry represent human efforts to choose priorities that are out of sync with the order God prescribes for human systems and relationships. Thus, when Micah links justice and steadfast love with humility (Mic. 6:8), he calls us to accept our true standing in relation to the God who is "exalted by justice" and before whom "the eyes of the haughty are humbled" (Isa. 5:15-16).

Acknowledging our spiritual poverty, we are ready to take the second step in developing the extreme virtue of justice. The next step is to nurture in our hearts a compassion for the poor and marginalized. Micah presents the unjust business leaders of his day as cold, calculating individuals.

> Alas for those who devise wickedness and evil deeds on
>   their beds!
> When the morning dawns, they perform it,
>   because it is in their power.
> They covet fields, and seize them;
>   houses, and take them away;
> they oppress householder and house,
>   people and their inheritance (Mic. 2:1-2).

The unjust don't have a problem exploiting others, giving no thought to the fellow humanity of their poor neighbors in light of their own gains. Their watchword resembles modern slogans like "there's a fool born every minute" and "never give a sucker an even break." Such callousness in Micah's day allowed injustice and dishonesty to pervade the entire economic system:

> Can I forget the treasures of wickedness in the house of
>> the wicked,
>> and the scant measure that is accursed?
> Can I tolerate wicked scales
>> and a bag of dishonest weights?
> Your wealthy are full of violence;
>> your inhabitants speak lies,
>> with tongues of deceit in their mouths (Mic. 6:10-11).

The results are simply inhuman:

> Listen, you heads of Jacob
>> and rulers of the house of Israel!
> Should you not know justice?—
>> you who hate the good and love the evil,
> who tear the skin off my people,
>> and the flesh off their bones;
> who eat the flesh of my people,
>> flay their skin off them,
> break their bones in pieces,
>> and chop them up like meat in a kettle,
>> like flesh in a cauldron (Mic. 3:1-3).

Micah is surely speaking metaphorically here, not accusing the leaders of actual cannibalism. The message is that injustice that devours the poor is as inhuman as cannibalism.

Such inhumanity is possible only when people fail to recognize the humanity of their oppressed neighbors.

So, a crucial step in practicing justice is appreciating the co-humanity of all people by having compassion for the poor and their plight. There is no place among God's people for callous attitudes that subject the poor to further inhumanity. Sadly, Christians in North America are often guilty of such callousness. We align ourselves with political ideologies that assault the poor by blaming them for their own poverty and advocating the withdrawal of all public support programs. Upper-middle-class Christians have no warrant for smugness or feelings of superiority because of the relative ease of their circumstances. A layoff, a bad investment, an accident, a major illness, or even a divorce can plunge a family suddenly into poverty. The old saying is right: there but for the grace of God go I. Those who do not have to wonder if there will be money for rent and groceries next month should be grateful and should open their hearts to those of God's children who are not so fortunate.

Compassion has to do with the dynamic character of biblical justice. Controversial ethicist Joseph Fletcher may have oversimplified matters when he said, "Love and justice are the same thing, for justice is love distributed." But justice and steadfast love are closely linked. According to Hosea, justice is connected to steadfast love as sowing is to reaping: "Sow for yourselves righteousness; reap steadfast love" (Hos. 10:12). Or, as it reads in the Contemporary English Version, "Plow your fields, scatter seeds of justice, and reap faithfulness."

The third step is action. Compassion for the poor should result in action on behalf of justice. Here is where the extreme virtue of justice is challenged. In the complex global economy our lives are enmeshed in, injustice is pervasive and seemingly intractable. The dollars we regularly spend at the department store cash register pay for the exploitation and oppression of workers oceans away whom we will never meet. Our grocery dollars subsidize the seizure of lands from peasant farmers in developing nations for the profit of multinational corporations. Disentangling ourselves from injustice in the global marketplace seems impossible. None of us can change the world. To sustain the virtue of justice, we need help from the virtues of courage and hope.

So it is good to begin with small steps, and there are many small steps we can take. Treat the low-wage service workers that you come into contact daily with as persons whose dignity is equal to your own rather than as servants or as mere cogs in the economic machine. Avoid humor that dehumanizes groups of people. Vote for candidates whose policies resemble the biblical standard of justice as compassion for the poor instead of only voting in terms of your own economic self-interest. When you do know of specific economic injustices, avoid supporting the businesses responsible. Volunteer at your local homeless shelter, food closet, or soup kitchen. Support charitable organizations that work on behalf of the poor. (While charity is no substitute for economic justice, it is consistent with compassion for the poor.) Support organizations that lobby for more just social policy. Teach your children the equality of all people. Combat materialism by buying second-hand goods. Through small steps such as these, we can grow toward having our lives characterized by justice.

Here's a simple test: When you see a news report about a group taking action against economic exploitation, how do you respond? What is your first gut reaction? If your first reaction is a wish—even a secret wish—that the poor would get their way, then the seeds of biblical justice have been planted in your heart and life. Perhaps you need to explore ways to take effective action, but your heart is in the right place. If your first reaction is confusion or boredom, you have some growing to do. You are in danger of developing the cold, callous attitude that makes injustice and inhumanity possible. If your first reaction is an angry wish that those bleeding hearts would stop causing trouble and accept the cold, hard realities of the marketplace, then you are either having a bad day or in serious need of repentance. Your attitude is the attitude of the haughty who will be brought low before the God who is exalted by justice.

Dynamic, restorative, biblical justice is about inclusion. All are equally children of God, all God's children bear the right to be included in God's family. People in our society are very fond of asserting our rights. But biblical justice calls us to renounce our rights and take on the vocation of servanthood. Rather than be consumed with my right to keep the money I worked for, biblical justice demands that I concentrate on my responsibility to promote the dignity and well-being of my neighbor—especially those neighbors who are destitute and outcast.

Once, when our younger daughter Hannah had been sent to her room for some small misbehavior, my wife and I were talking with our older daughter Hope. The three of us began playing a game that was normally part of very special family times when all four of us were present. Suddenly, Hannah cried out from her room, sobbing, "You're playing a family game, and I'm family!" Hannah was right. She was family, and whatever minor infraction she had committed could not take away the fact that she was family. So we hugged her, dried her tears, included her in the game, and discussed an alternative discipline for her earlier infraction. Restorative biblical justice is about including all members in the family of God's people.

In a complex global economy, devising strategies to implement justice are difficult. But the difficulty of the task is no excuse for despair. And the difficulty of the task is certainly no excuse for failing to develop the compassion that biblical justice entails. As Elie Wiesel stated in his 1986 Nobel Peace Prize lecture, "There may be times when we are powerless to prevent injustice, but there must never be a time when we fail to protest." None of us can change the world. But each of us can practice justice in our own relationships with other people. And each of us can do our part to bring justice to our families, our churches, our communities, and our world.

For Reflection and Action

1. Think about the ways you may participate unknowingly in unjust social and economic structures. For example, do you know anything about the working conditions of the workers who sewed the clothes you are wearing? Were the farm workers who picked the produce you had for dinner exposed to toxic pesticides? Were they paid and housed decently? Was the coffee you drank this morning grown on land seized from subsistence farmers and sold by corrupt officials to a for-profit corporation? It is difficult if not impossible to disentangle ourselves from the injustice of the global economy, but we can at least try, and we can repent and ask God's help and forgiveness when we fail.

2. Think about ways you may benefit unwittingly from racial injustice. For example, I have lived in houses that my landlord would refuse to rent to persons of a different skin color. Pray that God will help you be an instrument of racial justice.

3. Reflect on the meaning of "justification by grace." This means that we are justified (able to stand before God's

judgment) solely on the basis of God's free gift—nothing about what we do or who we are affects our standing before God. If God regards us without any reference to merit, then how should we regard others?

4. How effective is your church in supporting one another in the struggle for justice? How could your church or Bible Study group be more effective in providing encouragement and accountability in the struggle for justice?

5. What role(s) could you as an individual play in helping your church or group become a more effective instrument in the struggle for justice?

6. Review the list of suggestions for taking small steps toward living a more just life on page 55. Which of these or other steps do you already do? Which would you like to commit to? Add to the list and share your ideas with others in your church or group. A helpful book that can get you started is *Basic Trek: Venture into a World of Enough* by Dave Schrock-Shenk (Herald Press, 2002). This is a great book to use as a group, family, or individually and covers everything from economics to conservation of resources to simple living.

Prayer

God,
Our Advocate and Judge,
We acknowledge before you our spiritual poverty—
That we possess nothing with which we can justify
    ourselves.
We thank you that you justify us by your grace.
We confess to you our failure
To show our neighbors the compassion

You have shown to us.
We confess also that our lives are entangled
In systems of injustice and oppression.
Forgive us these sins of omission and commission;
Melt our hearts of stone.
Fill us with your compassion
So that your justice might flow though us
And flood our unjust world with hope.
Amen.

READ: HOSEA 2:2-23 AND 6:1-6

For I desire steadfast love and not sacrifice,
the knowledge of God rather than
burnt offerings.
—Hosea 6:6

four

STEADFAST LOVE

While we were sharing prayer concerns one evening, my younger daughter Hannah observed, "We need to pray for God, because God has to love everybody!" Hannah had inadvertently hit upon a couple of key truths about love in general and about God's love in particular. First, God's love is extremely large in scope. Second, love is hard work.

In the sixth chapter of Hosea, we find a dialogue between God and God's people, mediated by the prophet, on the nature of love and of God's demands. The people speak first:

> Come let us return to the LORD;
> for it is he who has torn, and he will heal us;
>> he has struck down, and he will build us up....
> Let us know, let us press on to know the LORD;
>> his appearing is as sure as the dawn;
> he will come to us like the showers,
>> like the spring rains that water the earth
>> (Hos. 6:1, 3).

In these verses, all seems well. The people have heard from Hosea the message of God's judgment on their unfaithfulness, and they are now ready to repent of their unfaithfulness and return and give their devotion to the Lord. All that's left is for God to accept their repentance and restore them to a state of blessedness, and everyone will live happily ever after.

But that's not how God responds. God is not quick to accept their repentance:

> What shall I do with you,
>   O Ephraim?
> What shall I do with you,
>   O Judah?
> Your love is like a morning cloud,
>   like the dew that goes away early (Hos. 6:4).

Wait a minute, God says. I've heard this song and dance before. I know you, and I know your ways. Your repentance is superficial. Your love is not a deep and abiding love. Your love is like the fog or the morning dew—it's refreshing while it lasts, but it evaporates quickly in the heat of the day. Such love is not the love God demands: "For I desire steadfast love, and not sacrifice, the knowledge of God rather than burnt offerings" (Hos. 6:6).

God demands *hesed*. Often translated mercy or loving kindness, *hesed* is best rendered steadfast love. *Hesed* is God's covenant love that is steadfast despite God's people's unfaithfulness, a love that does not wane or waver when times or circumstances change. *Hesed* is the essence of God's own character. And *hesed* is what God expects of God's people. So here we have an importance lesson about virtue in general and the virtue of steadfast love in particular: God's people are to model their character after God's own character. God is faithful to God's people, therefore, God's people are to be steadfast in their devotion to God and merciful in their dealings with one another. This is *hesed*—mercy, faithfulness, loving kindness, and steadfast love.

The first thing to be said about steadfast love is the obvious: steadfast love is steadfast. Steadfast love abides; it is seen in the ability to make and keep commitments. Steadfast love isn't extinguished with the winds of passion, isn't washed away in the ebb and flow of emotion. Steadfast love is an abiding faithfulness. It is precisely this lack of faithfulness that the prophets and other biblical writers condemn. The pattern that unfolds in history as told by the biblical writers is a cycle of God's people turning aside to worship other gods, falling under oppression by their enemies, crying out to the Lord and repenting of their unfaithfulness, and being restored to independence and blessedness. But then the cycle starts all over again. Once relative prosperity sets in, the unfaithfulness returns. Elijah challenges the people to stop wavering in their faithfulness: "How long will you go limping with two different opinions? If the LORD is God, follow him" (1 Kings 18:21). Steadfast love is abiding, consistent, and undivided. The prophets call on God's people to be unwavering in their devotion to God, just as God is unwavering in steadfast love.

If steadfast love is an abiding faithfulness, then it obviously involves more than mere emotion. When the prophets call for steadfast love, or when Jesus commands us to love our neighbor, they are not instructing us to have warm fuzzy feelings for one another. As Wendell Berry notes in *Sex, Economy, Freedom, and Community*, there is a difference between the feeling of love and the practice of love. The feeling of love, like all feelings, is unreliable. Feelings come and go. They change with changes in our external circumstances or in our body chemistry. They fade over time. Even in a healthy, lifelong marriage, the feeling of love ebbs and flows. That's why the practice of love is so important. The practice of love is simply doing loving things—consistently and habitually—whether or not the feeling of love is present. In a marriage or other close relationship, the practice of love cements the bond and helps maintain the relationship, not only through times of conflict, but also through the inevitable peaks and valleys in the feeling of love. When Scripture commands us to love, it is the practice of love that we are called to. We are to practice love as a virtue—habitually. We are to become loving people.

The abiding nature of steadfast love has implications for both spirituality and ethics. In our spiritual life, steadfast love means continuing to practice devotion through the ebbs and flows in our life of faith. We need to worship, pray, and read Scripture faithfully, avoiding the temptation to let our spiritual discipline slide when we get too busy or when things are going so well we don't see the need to take time to pray. We also must avoid the temptation to abandon our spiritual discipline in the darker times—when we feel that God is distant, when prayers seem to go unanswered, when we are at the receiving end of the injustice that often characterizes life in a sinful and fallen world.

There is room for us to be angry at God within the bounds of steadfast love. Like Jeremiah and Elijah, we can take our complaints to God rather than letting them become a wedge driven between us and our Maker. Steadfast love is a matter of commitment, and a true commitment to God will endure through the emotion-laden ebbs and flows in one's spiritual life.

With respect to ethics, the virtue of steadfast love means developing loving habits in the ways we relate to other people. The implications are clearest in intimate relationships such as marriage, parenting, or close friendship. But steadfast love as a virtue applies to all relationships. Steadfast love means treating people with kindness, compassion, and mercy. As abiding faithfulness, steadfast love implies that we will show integrity, loyalty, and dependability in how we relate to others. Needless to say, if we are living out the extreme virtue of steadfast love, our actions will be characterized by kindness, compassion, and integrity whether or not we happen to like the people to whom we relate.

God demands more than a good start and good intentions, Hosea says. God demands a deep, abiding faithfulness that stands the test of time. This, after all, is what it would mean to claim steadfast love as a virtue or character trait: steadfast love would be our characteristic way of acting—not just once, or now and then, but consistently over the long haul. The misty, easily evaporated love in Hosea 6:4 seems characteristic of so many people—so many Christians even—in our day and age. The problem with most people today, I think, is not that we intend to do wrong. Yes, a few people are genuinely wicked, with no concern for right and wrong or for the interests and well-being of others. But most people, I think, don't set out to do wrong. Most people intend to do good most of the time. Their intentions just aren't strong enough. Their intention to do good is like a morning cloud or the early dew, easily evaporated when the heat of the pressure of everyday living hits them. Too often, our intentions are only as strong as our emotions. Have you ever had something important you needed to do—you set aside time to do it, and really intended to—but when time came, just didn't feel like it (you were too tired, or too stressed, or too grumpy, or too depressed, or just found something else to do instead)?

God's steadfast love is not like that. Scripture bears witness over and over again to the abiding nature of God's steadfast love. In Exodus and Numbers, time and time again God's people complain against God and Moses, and act unfaithfully, and God's anger burns hot against them to the point that God intends to destroy them. But God's steadfast love always overcomes and tempers God's wrath, and God does not destroy God's people. Time and time again God sends prophets to warn the people and urge them to repent and avoid the judgment they deserve for forsaking their covenant with the Lord. The witness of Scripture is that God never abandons God's people no matter how many times God's people abandon God. That kind of steadfastness, that kind of consistency, is what God wants us to show in our lives—love, mercy, and faithfulness of a deep and abiding nature. Love, mercy, and faithfulness should be at the core of our personality and our character—so that if we were to do something inconsistent with steadfast love, others would say "That's not like him!" or "She's not acting like herself!"

Steadfast love is also intimately connected with knowledge of God. Hosea 6:6 is an example of the parallelism that is common in Hebrew poetry. In parallelism, two lines convey the same or similar meanings. Both lines of Hosea 6:6 contrast something God desires with something God rejects: "For I desire steadfast love and not sacrifice, the knowledge of God rather than burnt offerings." The two terms naming what God rejects, "sacrifice" and "burnt offerings," are synonymous. Therefore, the reader should infer that the two terms naming what God desires are also closely connected. Steadfast love and knowledge of God are intimately related.

Hosea's detailed description of the condition of God's people bears out the connection between knowledge of God and steadfast love; he links Israel's unfaithfulness with a deficiency in her knowledge of who God is and what God has done for her. "She did not know," Hosea says, speaking for God, "that it was I who gave her the grain, the wine, and the oil, and who lavished upon her silver and gold that they used for Baal" (Hos. 2:8). This describes a deficiency in knowledge of God: God's people have failed to understand that God is the source of the fertility of the earth and the fruits of agriculture; they incorrectly credit the gods of their Canaanite neighbors with having dominion over the land. In another passage, reminiscent of the covenant lawsuit theme of Micah, Hosea again links Israel's unfaithfulness with her failure to know God: "Hear the word of the LORD, O people of Israel; for the LORD has an indictment against the inhabitants of the land. There is no faithfulness or loyalty, and no knowledge of God in the land" (Hos. 4:1). Later, Hosea shifts from the image of Israel as unfaithful wife to the image of Israel as rebellious child. Here again, he links their sin to a deficiency in knowing God:

> When Israel was a child, I loved him,
>   and out of Egypt I called my son.
> The more I called them,
>   the more they went from me;
> they kept sacrificing to the Baals,
>   and offering incense to idols.
>
> Yet it was I who taught Ephraim to walk,
>   I took them up in my arms,
>   but they *did not know* that I healed them
>   (Hos. 11:1-3, italics added).

If a deficiency in knowing God is part of the diagnosis, it stands to reason that increased knowledge of God is part of the cure. Hosea employs a metaphor of marital reconciliation to describe the restoration of Israel to a right relationship with God, and names knowing God as an indicator that reconciliation has occurred: "And I will take you for my wife forever; I will take you in righteousness and in justice, in steadfast love, and in mercy. I will take you for my wife in faithfulness; and you shall know the LORD" (Hos. 2:19-20).

Reconciliation with God, then, includes a more complete knowledge of God. Jeremiah echoes Hosea's message and the imagery when he identifies knowledge of God as a central feature of the "new covenant." He promises:

> The days are surely coming, says the LORD, when I will make a new covenant with the house of Israel and the house of Judah. It will not be like the covenant that I made with their ancestors when I took them by the hand to bring them out of the land of Egypt—a covenant that they broke, though I was their husband, says the LORD. But this is the covenant that I will make with the house of Israel after those days, says the LORD: I will put my law within them, and I will write it on their hearts; and I will be their God, and they shall be my people. No longer shall they teach one another, or say to each other, "Know the LORD," for *they shall all know me*, from the least of them to the greatest, says the LORD; for I will forgive their iniquity, and remember their sin no more (Jer. 31:31-34, italics added).

Our common sense experience bears out this connection between knowledge of God and steadfast love. In any healthy relationship, the more we come to know the one we love, the more we love them. So it is in the relationship between God and God's people. The more we grow in knowing God, the more we are able to love God. This is true particularly because to grow in knowledge of God is to become more acutely aware of God's love for us. In the Bible and Christian history, those who know God best seem to love God most. As Paul states, "For to me, living is Christ and dying is gain" (Phil. 1:21). Deeper knowledge of God deepens our ability to imitate God and live lives that resemble God's steadfast love.

Finally, there is something paradoxical in the ways we express steadfast love in our relationships. In relation to God, steadfast love is exclusive. The love we owe to God cannot be shared with other gods or rival objects of desire. This is why marital unfaithfulness proved to be such a fertile metaphor for the relationship between God and God's people in the preaching of Hosea, Jeremiah, and other prophets. Faithfulness to God, like faithfulness in marriage, means forsaking all others. Jesus elucidates this principle when he says, "No one can serve two masters" (Matt. 6:24). A. W. Tozer once said, "The gravest question any of us can face is whether we do or do not love the Lord." If we do love God, then we love God wholeheartedly. The paradox is that, though steadfast love for God is exclusive, steadfast love when directed toward other people is inclusive. Our love for our neighbors is rooted in and reflects God's love for us and our neighbors. Since God loves us all equally, we are to exclude none of God's children from the embrace of steadfast love. The kindness and mercy God demands of us extends to all of God's children.

Obviously, we love most effectively those closest at hand—our spouse, children, families, close friends. Yet love is to be extended to all neighbors—even to our enemies. Here again, the connection between steadfast love and knowledge of God is essential. As we grow in knowing God more fully and becoming more completely and acutely aware of God's love for us, we grow also in our capacity to see as God sees and love as God loves. Just as a sponge can absorb only so much water before it is full and water begins to spill out, so we absorb God's love only to have it flow out from us to others. Steadfast love, the essence of God's character, becomes the essence of our character as well.

The most important thing to remember about the love we are called to is that it is to be *steadfast*. The extreme virtue of steadfast love is faithful, consistent, enduring, unshaken. Steadfast love is an everyday love—it is part of the fabric of everyday life. When Francis of Assisi was asked what he would do if he knew he had only a few hours or days left to live, he responded that he would go on tending his garden. True steadfast love is such that, if we were suddenly to become aware that our life was near its end, we would not feel any need to change our plans: we are already loving God with our whole hearts constantly, and loving our neighbors as ourselves every day.

Steadfast love is really the only proper response to the love God showers upon God's children. In his book, *Teach Me to Pray*, W. E. Sangster suggests that daily prayer should begin in adoration of God:

> Think on the greatness of God—the incredibility of it that He should hear us at all. Does not the wonder of it almost strike you dumb? Praise be to God that God is the God God is!

Indeed, that the infinitely good God should love us, despite our frailty and our faults, is a wonder! How can we respond except by loving God in return?

For Reflection and Action

1. Reflect on the fact that the God of the whole universe loves you. How does that make you feel?

2. How steadfast are you in your love for God? Does your love for God ebb and flow according to your emotional states? Do your obligations or activities distract you from loving God wholeheartedly?

3. Spiritual disciplines can help us be more consistent in our love for God. Journaling has recently grown in popularity as a spiritual discipline. Try keeping a spiritual journal for a month. Every day, write your thoughts and feelings about God and your spiritual life. Include negative feelings, remembering that honest love is "for better or worse." After a month, consider whether you think that your love for God is more steadfast as a result of the disciplined attention.

4. Make a list of the people you encounter everyday. Is your relationship with each of them characterized by steadfast love on your part?

5. How do you practice love as part of your everyday living? What loving habits do you admire in other people? What are specific loving habits that you would like to cultivate and practice more faithfully?

Prayer

God,
Our Redeemer and Friend,
We confess that we have often failed
To love you with our whole heart
And love our neighbors as ourselves.
Grant us grace
That we may love you steadfastly
And our neighbors compassionately
As you have loved us.
Amen.

READ: ISAIAH 61:1-11; JEREMIAH 31:23-34

From there I will give her vineyards,
and make the valley of Achor a door of hope.
There she shall respond as in the days
of her youth,
as at the time when she came out
of the land of Egypt.
—*Hosea 2:15*

Do not remember the former things,
or consider the things of old.
I am about to do a new thing;
now it springs forth, do you not perceive it?
I will make a way in the wilderness
and rivers in the desert.
—*Isaiah 43:18-19*

Return to your stronghold, O prisoners of hope;
today I declare that I will restore to you double.
—*Zechariah 9:12*

five

HOPE

the prophets were people of hope. They were "seers": they could see a vision of the future God intends for God's people. Their mission was to communicate that vision so God's people would adjust their actions accordingly. As we saw in our discussion of Hosea in chapter 2 and 4, God's intentions are that God's people live in faithfulness to God's covenant, and even judgment is meant not merely to punish, but to purify and restore. Hope is the ability to hold in our minds a vision of God's future and allow that vision to direct our lives. As biblical scholar Walter Brueggeman puts it, God's people have the vocation of "living towards a vision." God's people are to be people of hope.

We live in a world where authentic hope is difficult to come by. One of the driving forces in our culture is an uncritical trust in progress. We assume that more and bigger are better, and we are driven to higher and higher levels of consumption and dependence on technology. Even the church buys into the myth of progress. Church marketing is a prevailing trend. Church growth is so widely accepted as normative that one dare not express the belief that a church might grow in faithfulness to the gospel without growing numerically. Bigger is better, and larger attendance, no matter how it is acquired, is assumed to be a sign of God's approval.

Alongside this naïve hope in progress, an opposite trend has grown. Our media-saturated culture has produced a generation of cynics. Irony rules. Media savvy people don't trust any message from any medium. While suspicion of media messages is good, an all-encompassing cynicism leads logically to despair. So, awash in a sea of culture where the Scylla of naïve optimism looms opposite the Charybdis of cynical despair, Christians face the challenge of steering a course guided by authentic hope in God. What does such hope look like?

First, hope, like steadfast love, is closely connected with knowledge of God. In a passage we've looked at several times, Hosea links Israel's unfaithfulness to a deficiency in their knowledge of God: "She did not know that it was I who gave her the grain, the wine, and the oil. . . ." (Hos. 2:8). The people of Israel, of course, *should* have had intimate knowledge of the God who had been with them from their inception. "When Israel was a child, I loved him, and out of Egypt I called my son" (Hos. 11:1). God had not been distant and unknowable, but close and attentive. "I led them with cords of human kindness, with bands of love. I was to them like those who lift infants to their cheeks. I bent down to them and fed them" (Hos. 11:4). Yet somehow their knowledge of God had gone awry, and they mistook the God's blessings for benefits from serving Baal. They were now on the verge of bringing judgment upon themselves. Yet, beyond the impending judgment, "a door of hope" opens (Hos. 2:15); God's people will once again know God intimately.

We may wonder how a people among whom God had dwelt so intimately could lose their grasp of the knowledge of God. But the sad truth of biblical history is that for every true prophet who brought the word of the Lord to the people, there were dozens of false prophets who brought a different message and who claimed they had the true word from God. For example, when Amos, Hosea, Micah, and Jeremiah warned that God was about to bring judgment for Israel's sin in the form of defeat at the hands of Israel's enemies, any number of false prophets predicted that God would deliver Israel and instead bring judgment on the enemy (Mic. 3:5-7; Isa. 9:15; Jer. 14:13-16). Human nature then was much like it is now—we tend to believe what we want to hear. So most of the people believed the optimistic reports of the false prophets. In fact, when Jerusalem was destroyed by Nebuchadrezzar of Babylon, instead of repenting, the majority blamed the negative attitude of Jeremiah for the disaster and still refused to see their own wrongdoing (Jer. 38:4; 42:2-3).

Knowledge of God is not something we can take for granted. It took years of neglect for God's people to evolve to the condition addressed by Hosea: they no longer knew God personally and were unable to discern the true message of God from all the other messages they received. This is a lesson for us. Jesus said, referring to himself, "the sheep follow him because they know his voice" (John 10:4). But we don't just hear the call of God in a vacuum. The ability to discern what God expects of us, to imagine the future God has for us, depends on an ongoing, daily, intimate relationship with God. We must nurture our knowledge of God daily through prayer, meditation, reflection, Bible study, faithful living, repentance, confessing our sins, and bearing one another's burdens.

Rooted in knowing the God of steadfast love, authentic hope is stubborn. The biblical prophets were often tempted to despair. For example, at one instance in his ministry, Elijah despairs to the point that he prays for his own death: "It is enough; now, O LORD, take away my life, for I am no better than my ancestors" (1 Kings 19:4). Jeremiah, known as the weeping prophet because he often expresses deep discouragement, laments, "Why is my pain unceasing, my wound incurable, refusing to be healed?" Then he accuses God: "Truly, you are to me like a deceitful brook, like waters that fail" (Jer. 15:18). In another passage, he echoes Job: "Cursed be the day on which I was born! The day when my mother bore me, let it not be blessed! Why did I come forth from the womb to see toil and sorrow, and spend my days in shame?" (Jer. 20:14,18).

But neither Elijah nor Jeremiah give in to their despair. Elijah goes on to complete the work God called him to do and to prepare Elisha to be his successor. Jeremiah goes on to prophesy that even the destruction of Jerusalem will not prevent God from establishing a new covenant with God's people. Hope rooted in knowing the God of steadfast love perseveres through life's ups and downs. The author of Lamentations, traditionally believed to be the prophet Jeremiah himself, illustrates the stubbornness of hope. Lamentations was written after the destruction of Jerusalem by the Babylonians. The author surveys the damage and considers the sad fate of Judah's best citizens carried into exile. Jerusalem had been the city of God, where God's dwelling place on earth, the temple, was located. That God's own city could be destroyed had been unimaginable to all but the prophets and the few who listened to them. Now everything is gone. The center of God's people's national and religious life is destroyed. Considering this catastrophe, the author of Lamentations affirms:

The steadfast love of the LORD never ceases,
    his mercies never come to an end;
They are new every morning;
    great is your faithfulness.

"The LORD is my portion," says my soul,
      "therefore I will hope in him" (Lam. 3:22-24).

So stubborn is authentic hope that it survives even the worst imaginable calamity.

A few years later, during the exile, God speaks to the prophet Ezekiel in a valley of dry bones. "Can these bones live?" God asks. Ezekiel follows God's instructions to prophesy to the bones, and sees them take on sinew, flesh, and skin and come to life. This explanation is offered:

> Then he said to me, "Mortal, these bones are the whole
>   house of Israel. They say,
> 'Our bones are dried up, and our hope is lost; we are cut
>   off completely'" (Ezek. 37:11).

The exile was a debilitating experience. Surely many of the exiles felt that all hope was lost. But hope rooted in God's steadfast love endures, and God promises through Ezekiel and other prophets that God's people will be restored.

In my own struggles to follow my professional vocation while being faithful in my vocation as a father to my two daughters, I've often felt like my bones were dried up. I watched my children suffer because I left the full-time career path and took on the poverty of a graduate student. I then watched them suffer more because I took a position in a town that was not a healthy environment for them. I sent out dozens of résumés and applications only to receive form rejection letters. Hopeful job searches were canceled at the last minute due to "unforeseen budgetary constraints." Often, I've been tempted to give up. But then I think about how blessed I truly am. In his most pensive letter, Paul writes, "I am confident of this, that the one who began a good work among you will bring it to completion by the day of Jesus Christ" (Phil. 1:6), and "to me, living is Christ and dying is gain" (Phil. 1:21). God has indeed begun a good work among us. Authentic hope is not extinguished or even obscured by the trials—large or small—of everyday life.

Hope perseveres because it looks forward rather than backward. Time and time again, the prophets emphasize that God intends to do something new among God's people.

> Do not remember the former things,
>   or consider the things of old.
> I am about to do a new thing;
>   now it springs forth, do you not perceive it?
> I will make a way in the wilderness
>   and rivers in the desert (Isa. 43:18-19).

Jeremiah prophesies a new covenant. Ezekiel promises that God will put a new heart and a new spirit in God's people. As Jesus and the first Christians bring the prophetic witness forward to their own time, we see the new covenant theme expanded and we read of new wine and a new commandment. And Paul writes, "So if anyone is in Christ, there is a new creation: everything old has passed away; see, everything has become new!" (2 Cor. 5:17).

God's people must be open to new things God wants to do among us. Even though the prophets often remind God's people what God has done among them in the past, God's people are not to dwell in the past. Surely living in the past was a great temptation for the nation Israel. Not only did they have the collective memory of God's mighty acts, but the actual law of God written on two stone tablets sat in a wooden box in the temple. Moreover, God had covenanted with David to establish his throne forever in Jerusalem. If ever a people had reason to believe that God was finished communicating with them, it was the biblical nation of Israel/Judah.

This is one reason it was so easy to listen to all those false prophets who brought the familiar and comfortable message that God would never allow Jerusalem to be destroyed.

All religious folk share a great temptation to focus on what God has done in the past. Ironically, during the period of the exile, when the prophecy quoted above from Isaiah 43 probably originated, everything from the past that people were clinging to was gone. And yet the prophet has to implore, "Do not remember the former things, or consider the things of old." God says through the prophet: Forget about all that! Look forward to the new thing I am about to do! The prophet even expresses concern that if people remain focused on the past, they might not even notice the new thing God is about to do.

Christians, of course, are subject to the same temptation of dwelling on the past. Says Ralph Neighbor, the seven last words of the church are "We never tried it that way before!" If we focus on the past, we might miss out on whatever new things God wants to do among us. Authentic hope remembers how God has blessed us in the past and in the present, but keeps its focus on how God will bring the good work to completion in the future. Like the prophets, we need to catch a vision of the future God intends for us. Then we can structure our lives so that we are living toward that vision.

We need a vision. As individuals, we can ask, what would our life look like if God had absolute control? If all the blessings God wants to give us came all at once? Then we can hold that vision in our hearts and let it inspire us to take our next small step toward making that vision come true. As congregations—communities of faith—we can ask, what would we look like if God's Holy Spirit had absolute control of our life together? If all the blessings God wants to bestow on this congregation, and on this community through the ministries of this church, came true all at once? And we can hold that vision in our hearts, and evoke it in our worship and our service, and let it inspire us to take our next small steps toward making that vision come true.

A man walking in the park saw a young boy practicing archery. The boy pulled back the string and sent the arrow from the bow, then watched as the arrow traveled about three quarters of the distance to the target and fell to the ground. The boy pumped his fist and shouted, "Yessss!" The man was puzzled. The boy repeated the process, shooting another arrow only about three quarters of the distance to the target, this time jumping into the air and shouting "All right!" The man asked, "Why are you so excited? You're not even close to the target!" The boy replied, "Yeah, but this is a lot farther than I could shoot yesterday!"

One of the chief meanings of the biblical words for sin is to fall short, as when an arrow falls short of its target. In archery, you traditionally need to aim a little above the target to adjust for the effects of gravity. Too many times in life, we as God's people set our aim too low. We need a vision to aim toward, even if it is a vision we never quite reach. Like the boy in the story, we can celebrate being closer to our target than we were yesterday, and we can keep aiming high, trusting that, with God's help, we'll move even closer to our target tomorrow.

At times, it is easy to feel like a prisoner—trapped by the pressures, demands, and difficulties of life. So often we feel we have no control over what happens to us. Often it seems that the power to do what we want or need to do is beyond our grasp. Zechariah challenges us to think of ourselves as "prisoners of hope" rather than as prisoners of life's circumstances (Zech. 9:12). Authentic hope in God frees us to "rejoice in the Lord always" (Phil. 4:4). Hope enables us to pray with the Psalmist,

Why are you cast down, O my soul,
   and why are you disquieted within me?
Hope in God; for I shall again praise him,
   my help and my God (Ps. 42:5).

If we hold in our hearts a vision of the life God is moving us toward, we have a path by which we can escape the temptation to despair and be prisoners of hope instead.

A particular temptation to despair threatens those actively seeking to live out the extreme virtues we've been considering. Those who work for justice, for example, can easily be overwhelmed at the magnitude of the injustice that must be confronted. Those who live sacrificially find themselves working and living alongside ministers and alleged members of the community of faith who are self-serving and who promote self-indulgence. Those seeking to practice steadfast love encounter the fickleness of the faith and commitment of fellow believers. Those who strive to be peacemakers must confront the violence and vengefulness of fellow believers as well as their own violent and vengeful impulses. If even the faith community fails to produce large numbers of people living the virtues, is there any real hope?

Moreover, when churches and other religious institutions are guilty of heinous evil just like secular institutions, despair may really be the logical response. We must confront and resist this temptation to despair constantly. We must remember that evil results from the fallenness of creation, and that whatever is fallen can be redeemed. As my friend Michele Tooley notes in her book, *Voices of the Voiceless: Women, Justice, and Human Rights in Guatemala*:

Instead of giving up on evil systems, the Christian community must resist evil while recalling structures and systems to their original purpose. When Christian structures and systems are perpetrators of injustice and oppression, an individual or group must act as leaven to call the institution to repentance and a new way of acting.

Redemption may seem to come slowly, but all creation awaits redemption (Rom. 8:20-22). And God's people are called to be agents of redemption. We fulfill our calling to be agents of redemption and prisoners of hope through spiritual discipline. We must practice prayer, study, community, and other spiritual disciplines to keep our hope alive and to continue growing in the other extreme virtues.

Not long ago, over the course of a year, one of my daughters was hospitalized several times with what proved to be a difficult to diagnose but relatively minor illness. Her suffering and the uncertainty that accompanied it were extremely difficult for us as a family. But as we walked the halls of those huge hospitals, we saw people in the deepest throes of illness being wheeled to surgery, or to some diagnostic procedure, or back to their rooms. We saw families in waiting rooms whose loved ones would not leave the hospital alive. We saw children with chronic and terminal illnesses, children who will never enjoy many of the things most of us take for granted. I came to realize in a very concrete way what a blessing it is just to keep being able to breathe in and out! What a blessing to continue to be able to enjoy the love and warmth of one's family! What a blessing to continue to be able to enjoy the loving fellowship of God's people in a church like the one that loved us and prayed for us through the whole ordeal! What a blessing to have just one more day to move a little closer to that vision of God's future than I was yesterday!

God's people are people of hope, and our hope sustains us through all of life's circumstances.

For Reflection and Action

1. Make a list of things you hope for. Do not worry about whether your hopes are realistic or not. Describe what it would be like if each hope was realized.

2. Now examine the things on your list. Are they things that are worthy of the hope God calls us to? Are they consistent with living out the other virtues named in this book?

3. Now look at your list of hopes again. What are you doing to help these hopes be realized? What could you do?

4. What specific things tempt you to despair? How can you overcome the temptation to despair?

Prayer

God,
Our Hope and Guide,
You have begun a good work within us,
Among us, and around us.
Infect us with hope;
Fill our minds with a vision
Of your work coming to completion.
Keep us moving day by day,
Step by step, closer
To the fulfillment of your purposes
For us and for all creation.
Amen.

READ: 1 KINGS 19:1-16; JEREMIAH 1:1-19; JONAH 2:1-10

Surely God is my salvation;
I will trust, and will not be afraid,
for the LORD GOD is my strength
and my might;
he has become my salvation.
—Isaiah 12:2

Do not fear, or be afraid;
have I not told you from of old and declared it?
You are my witnesses!
Is there any god besides me?
There is no other rock; I know not one.
—Isaiah 44:8

six

COURAGE

being a prophetic witness in a hostile world requires courage. In his book *The Prophets of Israel*, conservative Baptist biblical scholar Leon Wood points out that nearly all of the biblical prophets exhibited tremendous courage in their own character. Consider Elijah, for example. What courage it took for Elijah to challenge the Baal cult and its powerful matron, the wicked Queen Jezebel! It likewise took courage for Elijah to confront King Ahab with messages of God's displeasure with his rule. And, when Elijah's own life was in peril because of his opposition to the royal court—when all seemed lost—Elijah showed courage in finding the strength to persevere.

Other prophets showed similar courage. Samuel showed courage as a boy in his willingness to convey God's heart-breaking message of judgment to his mentor Eli, and later in his willingness to take on the mantle of political and military leadership against the Philistines. Nathan showed courage in confronting King David with his sinfulness in the Bathsheba affair, and in his decisive action during Solomon's succession to the throne. Amos had the courage to enter hostile territory and preach an unwelcome message of God's judgment, offending powerful religious and political leaders. Isaiah had the courage to speak forthrightly to the king on sensitive matters of foreign policy with a perspective that contradicted popular opinion. Micah had the absolute gall to predict the unthinkable—that Jerusalem, the holy city, had lost God's favor and would be destroyed. Jeremiah had the courage to deliver a message that the authorities perceived as treasonous, and he suffered severely for it. Like Elijah, he found the strength to persevere in his mission when things seemed hopeless.

The prophets are indeed shining examples of courage in action. In fact, we can see courage as an ingredient to all the other virtues. It takes courage to live sacrificially and responsibly in a consumer culture. It takes courage to love steadfastly when forgiveness is repeatedly required, to act justly amid gross injustice, to maintain hope when situations seem hopeless, to be at peace in a restless and violent world. Courage, then, is desirable not only for its own sake, but also for its usefulness in strengthening the other virtues that characterize faithful living. While we may not be called on to confront kings or presidents with a message of God's judgment, we need courage to keep developing and living out the virtues we are to exhibit as God's people in a fallen world. Practicing extreme virtue requires courage.

Practically, courage is a virtue for which it is helpful to recall the Aristotelian standard of moderation. Courage doesn't mean the willingness to try anything. That is foolhardiness! True courage includes the willingness to admit our limitations. In the biblical accounts of God's calling the prophets, a common element is the prophet's sense of inadequacy for the job. Courage is better expressed in humility than in pride. Pop psychology has taught us to suspect that people who exude overconfidence to the point of arrogance are actually masking feelings of inferiority. We need the courage to admit our limitations and respond realistically to the challenges we face.

But awareness of our limitations is never accepted as an excuse for inaction. The hesitance of Isaiah, Jeremiah, and Ezekiel is answered with the promise of God's power and presence in their lives and work. The courageous admit their limitations and let God fill in the gaps. Micah contrasts himself with the false prophets of his day who were motivated by selfishness, prophesying for pay, and telling the people who pay them only what they want to hear (Mic. 3:5-7); he makes clear that what distinguishes him from these false prophets is his dependence on God's power. "But as for me, I am filled with power, with the spirit of the LORD, and with justice and might, to declare to Jacob his transgression and to Israel his sin" (Mic. 3:8). By God's power, Micah possessed the courage to speak forthrightly about the sins of God's people and their disastrous consequences, which would include the unimaginable tragedy of the destruction of Jerusalem. Many years later, when Jeremiah would be accused of treason for preaching a similar message, Micah's courage and integrity would be remembered as a precedent for Jeremiah's release (Jer. 26).

Courage has many facets. One aspect of courage is decisiveness. Elijah challenged the people of Israel: "How long will you go limping with two different opinions? If the LORD is God, follow him; but if Baal, then follow him" (1 Kings 18:21). Courage requires making decisions—most basically, deciding whom you will serve. Decisiveness also means the ability to act when action is called for. Martin Luther King Jr. once said, "The ultimate measure of a man is not where he stands in moments of comfort and convenience but where he stands at times of challenge and controversy." The prophets faced moments of challenge and controversy decisively, and they boldly stood and proclaimed God's message regardless of the consequences. The courageous are able to take similar decisive stands when challenged to do so.

On the other hand, I once received a greeting card with the inscription, attributed to playwright Anton Chekhov, "Any fool can survive a crisis. . . . It's the day-to-day living that wears you down." Sometimes we need courage just to keep putting one foot in front of the other. From time to time, I have struggled with depression. People with clinical depression often have difficulty finding the strength even to get out of bed in the morning. And, whether diagnosed with depression or not, all of us are potentially subject to what classic spiritual writers have called the dark night of the soul, a temporary but debilitating experience of God's silence or absence that tempts us to despair. Like Elijah and Jeremiah, we sometimes need the courage to keep going when there seems no reason to go on.

This kind of courage, like the courage to take uncompromising stands in times of crisis, is developed by nurturing our dependence on God. As the familiar words of Isaiah 40:31 promise, "those who wait for the LORD shall renew their strength, they shall mount up with wings like eagles, they shall run and not be weary, they shall walk and not faint." Notice the inverted order of the accomplishments: from flying, to running, to walking—from the spectacular to the mundane. Strength and courage from God ultimately serve the purposes of everyday living. This is what Elijah learned from the still, small voice on Mt. Sinai (1 Kings 19:12). Though Elijah might have wished or even expected that all would be made well through one dramatic display of God's power, Elijah received instead the commission and the sustenance to keep at his work day by day and over the long haul.

Courage also arises from the awareness that we aren't in the business of serving God alone. The times when Elijah and Jeremiah were tempted to give in to despair were times when they felt absolutely alone. "I have been very zealous for the LORD, the God of hosts," Elijah laments, "for the Israelites have forsaken your covenant, thrown down your altars, and killed your prophets with the sword. *I alone am left*, and they are seeking my life, to take it away" (1 Kings 19:10,14, italics added). Jeremiah expresses the bitter sense not only of being alone in relation to his contemporaries, but even of being abandoned by God:

> I did not sit in the company of merrymakers,
>> nor did I rejoice;
> under the weight of your hand I sat alone,
>> for you had filled me with indignation.
> Why is my pain unceasing,
>> my wound incurable,
>> refusing to be healed?
> Truly, you are to me like a deceitful brook,
>> like waters that fail (Jer. 15:17-18).

God's people make up a community that has covenanted to pursue God's will together. From the very beginning, according to the witness of the covenant community, God saw that "It is not good that man should be alone" (Gen. 2:18, NKJV). In the covenant community, God's people en*courage* one another. "Each one helps the other, saying to one another, 'Take courage!'" (Isa. 41:6).

Courage is relative to individual temperament and to the demands of varying situations. Some people are naturally shy. For them, initiating a simple conversation can be an act of great courage. As a teenager, I once stood in the middle of a department store for a half hour, and then left without buying the blue jeans I wanted because I was too shy to approach a sales clerk for help. Overcoming my shyness was a continuous struggle for much of my life. When I was a hospital chaplain, introducing myself to patients and their families to start a conversation took all the courage I could muster. Other people find one-on-one conversation as natural and easy as breathing, but quake with fear at the thought of public speaking. What courage means varies from person to person, from situation to situation. I read about a man who donated blood more than 200 times. Yet for people who fear needles and medical procedures, donating blood just once would be an act of courage.

All of us need courage. And all of us exhibit courage every day in ways that go unnoticed—ways that even we ourselves might not think of as courageous. People show courage in overcoming an addiction by sticking to recovery one day at a time. It takes courage, when with a group of co-workers or friends, to refuse to laugh at jokes that dehumanize groups of people. It takes even more courage to speak up and express our disapproval at such humor. We may need courage to say no to the demands of career advancement so we can invest more time and energy in our family. We may need courage to leave a comfortable job or home to accept an opportunity that offers greater fulfillment of our sense of calling. It takes courage to put our families at odds with the surrounding culture and our children at odds with their peers by limiting the amount of consumerism or violent media that we allow into our homes.

We could read the strange little book of Jonah, so different from the other prophetic writings in Scripture, as a case study involving several of the virtues that we have considered—along with their corresponding vices. For example, Jonah moves from refusal to answer God's call toward accepting the responsibility God lays upon him. In addition, Jonah must overcome his own bigotry to learn that justice means compassion for all God's many children. Jonah also provides a glance at the struggle between fear and courage. In a humorous scene, as Jonah is fleeing by sea in the opposite direction from where God has told him to go, the sailors who are transporting Jonah become delirious with fear at the storm God sends to interrupt Jonah's journey. They wake Jonah, who has been sleeping through the tumult, and draw straws to see whose fault it is that their little ship is in peril. The lot, of course, falls to Jonah, who explains his plight and informs them that the storm will cease if they throw him overboard, which they reluctantly do (1:4-16). Note the ironies in this little episode. First, Jonah flees to avoid God's call, but is unperturbed by a life threatening storm at sea. Second, the pagan sailors are prompted to seek divine help in their distress, but the prophet of the LORD sleeps through it.

After being thrown into the sea, Jonah is swallowed by a large fish (1:17). Then, from the belly of the fish, Jonah prays: "As my life was ebbing away, I remembered the LORD; and my prayer came to you, into your holy temple" (2:7). Notice that the verbs in Jonah's prayer are translated in the past tense. This prayer is in the form of a psalm of thanksgiving, which typically expresses gratitude to God for some deliverance from trouble. From the belly of the fish, Jonah prays as if his deliverance has already occurred.

Courage is often posited as the opposite of fear. In the midst of fearful situations such as Jonah's predicament in the belly of the fish, the courageous person dares to trust and hope in God despite being naturally afraid. Faith is also often posited as the opposite of fear, which suggests that courage and faith are closely intertwined. The New Testament book of Hebrews describes faith as "the assurance of things hoped for, the conviction of things not seen" (11:1). Faith, in other words, is its own evidence.

When Jonah felt his life ebbing away, he remembered God, and had the courage to trust that his prayer would reach God's dwelling place. Jonah had the faith to trust that his life would be preserved despite all evidence to the contrary. We may at times feel that our life is ebbing away. Or we may feel that our life is hurtling along so fast we can't keep up. Whatever our predicament, we can find the courage to trust that the God who has called us will continue to help us move toward our destination. We can shore ourselves up with the conviction that hope is still alive. We can have faith. Like the prophets, and like God's people in every generation, we can take courage.

For Reflection and Action

1. What is your biggest fear? Does this fear diminish your faith? How?

2. Does this fear prevent you from doing things that you ought to do? What?

3. Devise a plan for overcoming this fear in manageable steps. For example, if you had a fear of public speaking, a good start would be making an informal presentation to a small gathering rather than a formal speech to an audience of hundreds. Then, as your confidence grows, place yourself in more challenging situations. And pray for God to strengthen and encourage you each step of the way!

4. Do you have other fears that are obstacles to your faith and service? How might you meet those fears with extreme courage?

5. Are there people from history or in your life today that you admire for having overcome a fear? How did they do it? What can you learn from them?

Prayer

God,
Our Strength and our Help,
We are so small and so weak,
And the faith to which you call us is so large!
Take away our fear,
And fill us with courage and strength
That we may encourage one another
And serve others in your Name.
Amen.

READ: ISAIAH 2:1-4 AND 11:1-9

They shall beat their swords into plowshares,
and their spears into pruning hooks;
nation shall not lift up sword against nation,
neither shall they learn war any more.
—Isaiah 2:4

Blessed are the peacemakers, for they will be
called children of God.
—Matthew 5:9

If it is possible, so far as it depends on you, live
peaceably with all.
—Romans 12:18

seven

PEACE

Our world cries out for peace.

After the events of September 11, 2001, no one can deny the need for peace in our world. As horrendous as those terrorist acts were, we shouldn't let them obscure the reality that violence has been rampant in our world continually.

During the months in which I've been writing this book, the desperate need for peace has been evident around the globe. Israel has been engulfed in violent conflict. Violence has continued to flare in the Balkans, as has the decades-long civil war in Myanmar. Fighting among ethnic groups has erupted in Indonesia and the Philippines. The anniversary of the Columbine High School massacre has passed, along with the dedication of the memorial to the Oklahoma City bombing victims. International attention has been riveted on several high-profile court trials involving other cases of terrorism. Violent gangs control many inner city streets, while small-town and suburban kids wonder if their school will be the site of the next news-making killing. Major movies in the United States celebrate serial killers as heroes and I listen to my twelve-year-old daughter protest as I refuse to give her permission to see one of these "cool"

R-rated films with her friends. Several department store chains have announced that they will no longer carry the most violent of video games. But violence continues to rage in our society and around the world.

When Jesus said, "You will hear of wars and rumors of wars" (Matt. 24:6), he accurately described not only the revolutionary hotbed of first century Palestine in which he lived, but virtually all times and places in human history. One is tempted to concede that the biologists are right: violence and aggression are links to our evolutionary past. And yet, Scripture promises peace. And Scripture calls us to be peacemakers. Is this realistic? How?

In discussing the extreme virtue of hope, we saw the importance of holding in our hearts a vision of the future God intends. Peace, *shalom*, is the concrete content of the prophets' vision of God's future. Shalom, the Hebrew word for peace, means more than just the absence of violence. Shalom means wholeness or well-being—a state of affairs in which all of creation is functioning in a harmonious manner and God's purposes for creation are being fulfilled. Mennonite biblical scholar Perry Yoder describes shalom as "the Bible's word for salvation, justice *and* peace" (italics added). Shalom, peace, is God's intended order for God's creation.

Isaiah offers a compelling portrait of shalom in his poetic description of what has become known as the peaceable kingdom:

> The wolf shall live with the lamb,
>   the leopard shall lie down with the kid,
> the calf and the lion and the fatling together,
>   and a little child shall lead them.
> The cow and the bear shall graze,
>   their young shall lie down together;
>   and the lion shall eat straw like the ox.

The nursing child shall play over the hole of the asp,
    and the weaned child shall put its hand on the
    adder's den.
They will not hurt or destroy
    on all my holy mountain;
for the earth will be full of the knowledge of the LORD
    as the waters cover the sea (Isa. 11:6-9).

What are we to make of such a strange picture? Are we to take these verses as an actual prediction and expect that, in the last days (whenever they might be), predators will become herbivores and befriend their former prey and toddlers will play with venomous reptiles with immunity from harm? I think not. What Isaiah offers us here is not prediction, but vision—a poetic vision of what the world might look like if all of creation were under the sway of shalom, God's peace. It is a vision we can hold in our hearts as an inspiration as we seek to live our lives in a manner consistent with shalom, thus bringing whatever small corner of God's creation we have the power to influence more closely in line with the dominion of God's peace.

What does the extreme virtue of peace entail? I said that shalom is more than the absence of violence. But it certainly encompasses the absence of violence. The first task in developing the extreme virtue of peace, is to renounce violence. "Nothing provokes so much horror and opposition within the Jewish tradition as war," claims Elie Wiesel in his 1986 Nobel Peace Prize lecture. The prophets certainly view the absence of violent conflict as essential to God's ultimate reign over all the earth. Isaiah declares, "They shall beat their swords into plowshares, and their spears into pruning hooks, neither shall they learn war anymore" (2:4). The prophets invite us to envision a world without violence and then live toward that vision. While none of us can eradicate war from the face of the earth, each of us can eliminate violence from our own hearts and minds.

American Christians have made too easy a compromise with violence. We accept too quickly the premise that violence is inevitable in a sinful and fallen world. We condone war too uncritically when our nation goes to war. We accept it without question when politicians propose increases in our already astronomical level of government spending on the machinery of war (and we support politicians who advocate eliminating the minimal amount our government spends on compassionate justice for the poor!). We even congratulate ourselves for being realists who recognize that conflict is inevitable among nations. We accept violence as entertainment. We view violence and aggression as integral parts of sporting events, and sometimes even value aggression as a character trait. How can we be peacemakers if we actively condone violence?

Violence does not build character—at least not Christian character. And violence cannot bring peace. Violence only begets more violence. A peace enforced by violence and brute force is no peace at all, but a smoldering cauldron of anger and hate awaiting an opportunity to erupt into violence again. Remember, after all, that it was the *Pax Romana*, the brutal Peace of Rome, that killed Jesus. When Peter raised his sword to resist the arrest of Jesus, Jesus said, "Put your sword back into its place; for all who take the sword will perish by the sword" (Matt. 26:52). Popular opinion may insist that one must fight fire with fire; Jesus' way is to fight violence with love.

We must meet violence with love because the peace God gives is rooted in reconciliation. We have seen how Hosea described the relationship between God and God's people through a metaphor of marital unfaithfulness followed by reconciliation. The language Hosea uses to describe the reconciliation between God and God's people prefigures both Isaiah's peaceable kingdom and his swords into plowshares speech: "I will make for you a covenant on that day with the wild animals, the birds of the air, and the creeping things of the ground; and I will abolish the bow, the sword, and war from the land; and I will make you lie down in safety" (Hos. 2:18). Here, reconciliation with God makes way for peace, shalom, to fill the shared life of the community of God's people and spill over to all nations and even all creation.

Jeremiah also describes the relationship between God and God's people in terms of estrangement and reconciliation. Employing marital imagery similar to that of Hosea, Jeremiah compares the unfaithfulness of God's people to illicit promiscuity:

> If a man divorces his wife
>   and she goes from him
> and becomes another man's wife,
>   will he return to her?...
> You have played the whore with many lovers;
>   and would you return to me?
>   says the LORD (Jer. 3:1).

This indictment is followed by at least three invitations for God's people to turn from their unfaithfulness and be reconciled with God:

> Return, faithless Israel,
>   says the LORD.
> I will not look on you in anger,
>   for I am merciful,
>   says the LORD;
> I will not be angry forever.
>   (Jer. 3:12; see also 3:14; 3:22; and 4:1)

Again following Hosea, Jeremiah describes the promised reconciliation between God and God's people as a "new covenant," unlike the former covenant, "a covenant that they broke, though I was their husband, says the LORD" (Jer. 31:31-32). Here is the message of the prophets in a nutshell: God's people have broken the covenant and are estranged from God; nevertheless God desires reconciliation that will bring peace.

The prophets also describe the reconciliation between God and God's people as resembling that between a parent and a wayward child (Hos. 11:1-9; Jer. 3:19 and 31:9; Isa. 63:7-17). God's love is presented as being undeterred by human rebellion. God is always seeking reconciliation with God's rebellious children. Jesus brings this view of God into the Christian era in his parable of the prodigal son, who, upon returning to his father's house, found grace and reconciliation rather than the judgment he deserved (Luke 15:11-32).

The first step in developing the extreme virtue of peace, then, is reconciliation with God. Reconciliation with God, however, is inseparable from reconciliation among God's people. The prophets condemned injustice as harshly as they did because injustice is a failure to recognize that the poor are part of the community of God's people. Injustice divides God's people. The relationship with God and the relationships among God's people are two sides of the same coin. As biblical scholar James D. G. Dunn explains,

> In Hebrew thought, it would not be possible for someone to be righteous apart from, without reference to that individual's responsibility toward others; it would not be possible to be righteous before God while remaining in unjust relationships with fellow human beings.

Jesus has this intimate connection between reconciliation with God and reconciliation with one's neighbor in view when he advises, in his Sermon on the Mount, that if one is estranged from a neighbor, one must go and be reconciled before bringing an offering to God (Matt. 5:24).

The clearest statement of the connection between peace as reconciliation with God and reconciliation among God's people is found in Ephesians, where Paul portrays reconciliation between Jewish and Gentile Christians as central to the work of Christ:

> But now in Christ Jesus you who once were far off have been brought near by the blood of Christ. For *he is our peace*; in his flesh he has made both groups into one and has broken down the dividing wall, that is, the hostility between us (Eph. 2:13-14, italics added).

In the early church, much conflict arose between Jewish Christians and Gentile Christians. Paul saw this conflict as a threat to the integrity of the gospel. After all, one of the earliest formulations of the basic message of Christianity is the expression of unity in the baptismal formula in Galatians 3:28: "There is no longer Jew or Greek, there is no longer slave or free, there is no longer male and female; for all of you are one in Christ Jesus." In Christ, the barriers of race, class, and gender that divide people are abolished. In Christ, we are reconciled with one another.

Reconciliation among God's people was so important, and division in the church so dangerous, that Paul made a very radical move to try to make peace between the two factions. Throughout his letters, Paul mentions a collection he is taking among the predominantly Gentile churches in Asia Minor and Greece for the poor, predominantly Jewish Christians in Jerusalem. Paul closes his letter to the

Corinthians with his initial plans for the delivery of this gift: "And when I arrive, I will send any whom you approve with letters to take your gift to Jerusalem" (16:3). When he wrote 1 Corinthians, Paul's plan is clearly to *send* the gift to Jerusalem (though he does add in the next verse, "If it seems advisable that I should go also, they will accompany me"). By the time he writes Romans, however, Paul's plans have changed. "I desire, as I have for many years, to come to you when I go to Spain," Paul writes to the Romans. "At present, however, I am going to Jerusalem in a ministry to the saints; for Macedonia and Achaia have been pleased to share their resources with the poor among the saints at Jerusalem" (Rom. 15:23-26). Here Paul intends to deliver the gift himself, not send it.

This is no minor change in plans. Travel in the ancient world was not as simple as gassing up the car and heading down the interstate or buying plane tickets on the Internet. A return to Jerusalem was a long, perilous journey. Moreover, according to Acts, Paul was warned before the trip that a visit to Jerusalem could mean his arrest and possibly even his execution (Acts 21:7-14). Why undertake such a risky journey? Because Paul was engaged in a ministry of reconciliation! The rift between Jewish and Gentile Christians was so severe, and the need for reconciliation so essential to the integrity of the gospel, that Paul felt the need to deliver the peace offering in person.

Notice also what Paul must give up in order to undertake this mission of peacemaking and reconciliation. In the verses from Romans 16 quoted above, Paul expresses a desire to visit Rome on his way to Spain. Carrying the gospel all the way to Spain—the edge of the known world and therefore the ends the earth—was the most far-reaching goal of Paul's missionary endeavors. But the westward expansion of the gospel movement would have to wait. *Paul's entire evangelistic/*

missionary enterprise is put on hold in order to make peace between Jewish and Gentile Christians. Reconciliation among God's children is central to the New Testament gospel; it must be a priority among God's people seeking to live out the extreme virtue of peace.

Since Paul's day, the Christian movement he so earnestly sought unity for has splintered into thousands of denominations and sub-groups. In our own day, conflict between denominations is a cause for concern, but conflict within denominations is more troubling. I cannot even imagine convincing a roomful of pastors in my denomination to put our entire missionary/evangelistic/church growth enterprise on hold to be reconciled with one another. I suspect the same holds true in most Christian denominations.

And yet, amid numerous conflicts and divisions, new seeds of reconciliation are sprouting among God's people throughout the world. In denominations most torn by conflict, small groups of concerned people from both sides are meeting to pray and seek common ground. Peace and justice networks are creating new types of unity across denominational lines among believers committed to ministries of reconciliation. And the restorative justice movement, led by the historic peace churches, is taking the good news of reconciliation beyond the walls of the community of faith and into what is certainly the arena where human relationships are at their most fractured—the criminal justice system. There are indeed places where believers who are seeking diligently to live out the extreme virtues of peace, justice, and steadfast love can connect and serve.

Finally, and most basically, an extreme virtue of peace includes peace within oneself. We have seen throughout this book that the prophets' focus was often on social, political, and economic situations. But they didn't ignore the inner life. Out of his own inner distress, Jeremiah repeatedly pours out his soul to God. Jonah cries out in distress from the belly of the fish. Their cries meet with God's peace. Isaiah describes the peace available to those who trust in God: "Those of steadfast mind you keep in peace—in peace because they trust in you" (Isa. 26:3).

The first Christians were marked and distinguished from their pagan neighbors by their inner peace or serenity. They were able to defy the codes of honor and shame that defined their social setting and even to face death without fear because they had experienced "the peace of God, which surpasses all understanding" (Phil. 4:7). Paul's answer to the charge that peace is unrealistic is to acknowledge the incredulity of the promise of peace but confirm the promise anyway. "Then, because you belong to Christ Jesus," Paul writes to the Philippians, "God will bless you with peace that no one can completely understand. And this peace will control the way you think and feel" (Phil. 4:7, CEV). Here we see the extreme virtue of peace in a nutshell—God's incomprehensible peace controlling the way we think, feel, and act.

The prophets envision a covenant community of shalom—a community of people at peace with God, with themselves, and with one another. Moreover, his faithful, peaceable community is to be so filled with shalom that God's peace overflows from them and extends to the nations and even to all creation. We who make up the covenanted yet broken community of God's people in the fragmented and war-torn world of the twenty-first century must try harder to absorb and reflect God's peace. We must nurture in our own heart and minds and life together a vision of a world in which God's peace reigns, and we must live as if our lives are moving toward that vision.

For Reflection and Action

1. The psalmist's admonition to "Pray for the peace of Jerusalem" (Ps. 122:6) reminds us that peacemaking begins with prayer. Make it a habit to pray for peace in our world and name specific places where violence looms. Praying for peace concretely serves two purposes. First, it breaks our self-centered habit of petitioning God only on behalf of ourselves and our small circle of friends and loved ones, helping us grow in awareness of our connection with the body of Christ around the world. Second, it opens the door to hope that peace can become a reality: we do not pray for things we consider impossible.

2. Combining a focused breathing exercise with a Scripture like Isaiah 26:3 produces a form of prayer that helps nurture inner peace. As you inhale slowly, recite silently the first half of the verse: "Those of steadfast mind you keep in peace." Then, as you exhale slowly, silently recite the second phrase: "in peace because they trust in you." Continue to repeat this procedure, concentrating only on your breathing and on the words you silently recite. Relax and allow God's peace to fill your heart and mind. Other passages of Scripture work in this exercise—for example, "The LORD is my shepherd / I shall not want" (Ps. 23:1), "those who wait for the LORD / shall renew their strength" (Is. 40:31), "I can do all things / through him who strengthens me" (Phil. 4:13). Try it with your favorite passage.

3. Raising children to be peaceful and peacemakers is a daunting challenge for parents and for anyone who cares for children. Toys, entertainment media, games, and the school cultures where our children spend most of their time are all saturated with violence. *Raising Peaceful*

Children in a Violent World by Nancy Lee Cecil offers many practical ideas and activities, as does the classic *Parenting for Peace and Justice* by James and Kathleen McGinnis, and the new edition of *How to Teach Peace to Children* by Anne Meyer Byler. An excellent resource covering all the passages of family life from the perspective of shalom is *Freedom Fences: How to Set Limits That Free You to Enjoy Your Marriage and Family*, by Gerald W. Kaufman, L. Marlene Kaufman, Anne Kaufman Weaver, and Nina Kaufman Harnish.

Prayer
God,
Our Shelter and Shield,
We pray for peace in Jerusalem,
In Jakarta, in Rangoon, in Sarajevo,
In Kigali, in Baghdad, in Kabul,
In Bogota, in Chiapas, in Groznyy,
In Moscow, in Pyongyang, in Beijing,
In Miami, in Newark, in Detroit—
Wherever violence threatens
We pray for peace;
We pray for peace in our neighborhoods,
In our schools, in our homes,
And in our hearts,
In the name of the One who is our Peace,
Amen.

Sources

Introduction

Anscombe, G. E. M. "Modern Moral Philosophy." In *Ethics, Religion, and Politics: The Collected Philosophical Papers of G. E. M. Anscombe,* vol. III. Minneapolis: University of Minnesota Press, 1981.

Aristotle. *Nichomachean Ethics.* Translated by Martin Ostwald. Indianapolis: Bobbs-Merrill, 1962.

Blenkinsopp, Joseph. *A History of Prophecy in Israel.* Rev. ed. Louisville: Westminster John Knox Press, 1996.

Hauerwas, Stanley. *The Hauerwas Reader.* Edited by John Berkman and Michael Cartwright. Durham, N.C.: Duke University Press, 2001.

Jones, W. T. *A History of Western Philosophy.* New York: Harcourt Brace & Company, 1952.

McIntyre, Alisdair. *After Virtue.* South Bend, Ind.: University of Notre Dame Press, 1981.

Pixley, Jorge. *Biblical Israel: A People's History.* Minneapolis: Fortress Press, 1992.

Rachels, James. *The Elements of Moral Philosophy.* 3d ed. New York: McGraw-Hill College, 1999.

Chapter 1

King, Martin Luther. *Strength to Love.* Philadelphia: Fortress Press, 1963.

Chapter 2

Barnette, Henlee. "Biomedical Ethics: A 'Now' Christian Concern." *The Western Recorder* 152 (8 March 1978): 5.

Etzioni, Amitai. *The Spirit of Community.* New York: Crown Publishers, 1993.

Niebuhr, H. Richard. *The Responsible Self.* San Francisco: HarperSanFrancisco, 1978.

Chapter 3

Fletcher, Joseph. *Situation Ethics*. Philadelphia: Westminster Press, 1966.

Heschel, Abraham Joshua. *The Prophets*. New York: Jewish Publication Society of America, 1962.

Sider, Ronald J. *Just Generosity: A New Vision for Overcoming Poverty in America*. Grand Rapids, Mich.: Baker Books, 1999.

Stassen, Glen. "Narrative Justice as Reiteration." In *Theology Without Foundations: Religious Practice and the Future of Theological Truth*. Edited by Stanley Hauerwas, Nancey Murphy, and Mark Nation. Nashville: Abingdon Press, 1994.

Wiesel, Eli. "Hope, Despair, and Memory." Nobel Lecture. December 11, 1986.

Zimmerli, Walther. *The Old Testament and the World*. Translated by John J. Scullion. London: SPCK, 1976.

Chapter 4

Berry, Wendell. *Sex, Economy, Freedom, and Community*. New York: Pantheon, 1992.

Sangster, W. E. *Teach Me to Pray*. Nashville: The Upper Room, 1959.

Verploegh, Harry, editor. *A. W. Tozer: An Anthology*. Camp Hill, Pa.: Christian Publications, 1984.

Chapter 5

Brueggeman, Walter. *Living Toward a Vision: Biblical Reflections on Shalom*. New York: United Church Press, 1982.

Neighbor, Ralph. *The Seven Last Words of the Church: We Never Tried It That Way Before*. Grand Rapids, Mich.: Zondervan, 1973.

Tooley, Michele. *Voices of the Voiceless: Women, Justice, and Human Rights in Guatemala*. Scottdale: Pa.: Herald Press, 1997.

Chapter 6

King, Martin Luther. *Strength to Love*. Philadelphia: Fortress Press, 1963.

Wood, Leon J. *The Prophets of Israel*. Grand Rapids, Mich.: Baker Books, 1979.

Chapter 7

Byler, Anne Meyer. *How to Teach Peace to Children*. 2d ed. Scottdale, Pa.: Herald Press, 2003.

Dunn, James D. G. "The Justice of God: A Renewed Perspective on

Justification by Faith." *Journal of Theological Studies* 43 (1992): 1-22.

Kaufman, Gerald W. et al. *Freedom Fences: How to Set Limits That Free You to Enjoy Your Marriage and Family.* Scottdale, Pa: Herald Press, 1999.

McGinnis, James and Kathleen. *Parenting for Peace and Justice.* Maryknoll, N.Y.: Orbis Book, 1981.

Roberts, Patricia L. *Raising Peaceful Children in a Violent World.* San Diego: LuraMedia, 1995.

Yoder, Perry B. *Shalom: The Bible's Word for Salvation, Justice, and Peace.* Newton, Kan.: Faith & Life Press, 1987.

The Author

David Fillingim teaches religion and philosophy at Shorter College in Rome, Georgia, and is a former pastor and hospital chaplain. He received his Ph.D. in Christian Ethics from Southern Baptist Theological Seminary in Louisville, Kentucky. He is the author of *Redneck Liberation: Country Music as Theology* (Mercer University Press, 2003).